SWEEPING THE BLUES AWAY

A Celebration of the
Merseysippi Jazz Band

Spencer Leigh

First published in Great Britain in 2002
ISBN 1 898806039

SWEEPING THE BLUES AWAY
A celebration of the Merseysippi Jazz Band

FORDEWOLD from Professor Stanley Unwin..........Page   3

FURTHER FOREWORD from Hunter Davies ....Page   4

INTRODUCTION ....Page   6

CHAPTER 1
I PUSH THE FIRST VALVE DOWN............................Page   8
Jazz: the first 50 years

CHAPTER 2
THE MUSIC GOES ROUND AND ROUND ....Page   37
Liverpool - UK jazz to 1950

CHAPTER 3
AND IT COMES OUT HERE ....Page   48
Formation of Merseysippi Jazz Band

CHAPTER 4
TEMPLES AND IDOLS ....Page   65
The Temple - Louis Armstrong in Liverpool

CHAPTER 5
UNDERGROUND MOVEMENT ....Page   86
Cavern - Clinton Ford

CHAPTER 6
IS THAT YOUR VINYL ANSWER?...............................Page 103
Esquire Records

CHAPTER 7
TRAD MAD...Page 111
Mardi Gras - Trad boom

CHAPTER 8
BACK O' TOWN BLUES...Page 124
Liverpool residencies - Jill Martin

CHAPTER 9
OH, YOU CALIFORNIA .... Page 136
Sacramento Jazz Festivals

CHAPTER 10
CLOSING TIME? .... Page 142
Hartley's - Today's repertoire

CONTRIBUTORS .... Page 154

APPENDIX 1 - PERSONNEL .... Page 161

APPENDIX 2 - VENUES .... Page 163

APPENDIX 3 - DISCOGRAPHY .... Page 165

I COULD WRITE A BOOK - BIBLIOGRAPHY .... Page 174

FORDEWOLD
from Professor Stanley Unwin

Merseysippi Jazz Band starty-ho in 19 forty-nilo. Let's face it, a real survivey-ho, the youngest being a mere fifty-several.

It's also the oldest of a two-trumpey-blow from inspire by Louis Armstrode of the ombouchure and joyful blasty top C to the earfolders. Oh yes. I believe Louis carried King Oliver's trumpy-blow.

Sacramento's HIGHS were an experience joyfold. Present residenters is at the Aigburth Arms and manyfold are the old turners up to enjoy their spesslodeof the jazzy-how. Indeed.

This Tome-Comprehensers is publicool by the Institute of Music Populade University of Liverpool which is a joy top know for all eardroves.

We shall hear among manyfold the Clinton Ford fine focus in the thrucus. What a throcal joy!

Thankit muchfolders to ask for unwy-wordage type thinggold and DEEP JOY.

Now for something sensibold from Hunter Davies.

Stanley Unwin

3

FURTHER FOREWORD
from Hunter Davies

Like most people of my generation, born 1936, I grew up with jazz being fashionable. Fashionable amongst fashionable people, old and young, who enjoyed a veneer of being in touch, rather bohemian, racy, daring, subversive, intellectual, part of an exclusive cult. Jazz gave them all that, or so it appeared.

In Carlisle, I used to go along and listen to Micky Potts and his Gateway Jazz Band, feeling I was in with the in. At Durham, as a student, we played Ken Colyer all the time in the JCR. One of the first people I ever interviewed as a grown up journalist was Chris Barber. Such a thrill.

Popular music of the time, when we were still growing up , back in the early 1950's, was strictly slush, ballads sung by crooners, silly ditties performed in a mid Atlantic accent, enjoyed by mums and shop girls. We student types hummed along as well, of course, but in private. What else was there to hum. But following jazz, apart of course from it being enjoyable, did convey a certain status and acceptability.

The arrival of skiffle and rock'n'roll changed all that, seducing away younger people from jazz, mostly for ever. When they first collided, there was a certain amount of hatred. The jazz people, in their jazz clubs, sneered at the amateur skiffle players, scruffs, who couldn't play anything properly. Skiffle players, like John Lennon, sneered back in return, dismissing all jazz music, mocking jazz fans for being boring people who wore Marks and Spencer pullovers.

And yet skiffle owed a lot to jazz. They do share musical roots, in the US and the UK. Paul McCartney's dad Jim, back in the 1920's, played in a Liverpool jazz band.

The existence of the Cavern Club in Liverpool, founded as a jazz venue, with the Merseysippi Jazz Band being the opening group, was vital to the development of the Quarrymen and then the Beatles.

While the Beatles went on into the stratosphere, local Liverpool jazz bands, such as the Merseysippi, trundled on, playing away, if rather quietly, in a corner, on their own.

They still are, over fifty years after they first began. It's remarkable how they have continued, still as semi amateurs, still enjoying themselves and bringing pleasure to many.

I suspect that if John Lennon had lived on, he might today have some nicer things to say about jazz, realising how much a part of musical history it is and, in the case of the Merseysippi Jazz Band, what a part it has played in the cultural and social and musical life of Liverpool over the last half century.

Spencer Leigh has done an extremely worthwhile job in recording their story and giving us a fascinating slice of oral history. Nice.

Hunter   *Davies*

Good luck with it
— Hunter

SWEEPING THE BLUES AWAY
A celebration of the Merseysippi Jazz Band

INTRODUCTION

In intellectual terms, 'Sweeping The Blues Away' offers a social history of jazz in Liverpool in the second half of the 20th century. It may be an important document as it hasn't been recorded at length anywhere else. But who cares? I wrote this book because I enjoy the Merseys' company and I love watching them perform. They play the happiest music I have come across and appear to be among the most contented individuals I've ever met. If there is any rancour or angst in their midst, they keep it very well hidden.

My thanks to all the current members of the Merseysippi Jazz Band and several past ones for talking to me, first in connection with four special editions of BBC Radio Merseyside's 'On The Beat' which celebrated the band's 50th anniversary in 1999 and then, in greater depth, for this book. I have also spoken to a host of jazz musicians, critics and fans and all the numbered quotes relate to our conversations. Again, my thanks to all.

What could be better than forewords from Stanley Unwin (still crazy after all these years) and Hunter Davies, who has authorised biographies of the Beatles and the Quarry Men amongst his many credits? My especial thanks to John Lawrence who let me trawl through the Merseys' archives for illustrations and press cuttings and to Derek Vaux who scanned them into the computer. Yet more thanks to Tim Adams, Geoffrey Davis, Anne Leigh and Mick O'Toole who have seen the text in one or more of its various stages.

I am very grateful to David Horn and Mike Jones of the Institute of Popular Music at the University of Liverpool for their belief in this project. David is the Director of the IPM and I thank him and his secretary, Debbie Ellery for the time they have devoted to it. We both thank the Friends of the University of Liverpool for their support and I hope that this is a credit to the excellent Liverpool Sounds Series.

Finally, I would also acknowledge my conversations with Kate

Smith whose thesis, 'Three Moments Within The Merseysippi Jazz Band', was completed in May 2001 and can be found in the IPM's library. She went to several of the MJB's nights at the Aigburth Arms and comments, "While I was carrying out my research, I was consistently the youngest audience member and, in fact, the only 'young person' there." In length of existence maybe, but playing jazz has kept the Merseys young and they are, by no means, typical pensioners. As you are about to find out.

Spencer Leigh
December 2001

Another Interview done—Clinton Ford and Spencer Leigh

CHAPTER 1
I PUSH THE FIRST VALVE DOWN
Jazz: the first 50 years

Roughly speaking, this chapter is a history of jazz up to 1949, the year that the Merseysippi Jazz Band was formed. However, I am omitting categories (bebop, avant garde, modern) and performers (Stan Kenton, Charlie Mingus, Dave Brubeck) with little influence on the ensemble. Also, when listing key recordings by the main performers, they are usually tunes that are also in the Merseys' repertoire.

I am fully aware that the history of jazz is a controversial subject and I have no urge to enter into the debate. This chapter simply gives details of the performers who are particularly relevant to an understanding to the Merseysippi Jazz Band. If you want to cut to the chase, start at Chapter 2.

I

Jazz music is often associated with prostitutes, gamblers, drunks and drug addicts, but there is a bad side. Those links go though its history and are still around today.

In the 17th century, the French had control of Canada and the Great Lakes. The explorers appreciated that the vast continent was drained by the Mississippi and its many tributaries. The river was the logical way to move people and goods across North America and down to the Gulf. The French wanted to establish a port around the mouth of the Mississippi, but knew they would have to build it on swamps. To add to the problem, the area was prone to both hurricanes and excessive heat.

So, New Orleans was founded by the French in 1718 and the Duc d'Orleans, the regent to Louis XV, approved a company for selling shares in the project to a gullible French public. The shareholders would receive dividends once the port was thriving and once, so they said, gold was discovered. There was no gold, the shareholders became disillusioned and the company collapsed in 1720. If the French government had thought it through, this could have been a profitable enterprise. Instead, for many years, New

Orleans was a town of wooden houses and muddy streets.

The French were wary about who might live in New Orleans. When they claimed Louisiana, there were only a few thousand Choctaw Indians in the area. Distrusting both the English and non-Catholics, they chose French Catholics as settlers, but what French Catholics. Someone had the ridiculous notion of offering freedom to male prisoners if they would settle in New Orleans and offering prostitutes household goods if they would help the men to settle down. No such luck. Let loose in Louisiana, the prisoners continued with their antisocial practices and the prostitutes still sold their bodies. Nevertheless, New Orleans did slowly develop and slaves were imported from Africa to help with labour shortages.

Following the Seven Years War, France was forced to cede New Orleans to Spain in 1763, although the inhabitants, now numbering 5,000, were reluctant to accept the new ownership. Because of its position, the British colonies in North America wanted links with New Orleans, but the Spanish government distrusted the British even more than the French and revoked their trading rights.

The Declaration of Independence established America in 1776. The Americans quickly increased the trade in New Orleans, and the Spanish government offered trading benefits to Americans who accepted Spanish citizenship. Few Americans took up this offer, but they did settle in New Orleans. A widespread fire in 1788 destroyed many buildings, and most of the older buildings remaining in New Orleans are Spanish.

Napoleon recaptured Louisiana for the French in 1802, but his difficulties in financing wars at home caused him to sell the whole of Louisiana, including New Orleans, to the United States in the following year. New Orleans' population was then 8,000: 3,000 white, 3,000 coloured freemen and 2,000 coloured slaves.

New Orleans became crucial to the United States and, indeed, to world economy. It started growing faster than any other American city, and by 1830 only New York and Baltimore were larger. Surprisingly there was not much shipbuilding in New Orleans, but the city did become a financial centre. There was trade in furs, timber, sugar and cotton. By 1860 the population of New Orleans had risen to 170,000. 78,000 had been born in America and 66,000 were immigrants (Irish, German, French, British and Spanish). There were 14,000 slaves and 10,000 coloured people who were free.

There is some similiarity between the American Civil War and the current debate on Britain's role in Europe. The southern states did not want to follow laws created by the Union. They wanted the right to secede but unlike today, the most contentious issue was the continuation of slavery. After the war, four million slaves were freed, theoretically with 40 acres and a mule, although few of them saw that. Many southern whites did their best to make their lives intolerable. They were denied human rights and subjected to violence. What work they could find was little better than slavery.

In passing, it is worth noting that Robert E. Lee was the Confederate Army general who was the South's military leader during the American Civil War. After several victories, he was defeated at Gettysburg in 1863 and when he surrendered in 1865, the war was over. His name lived on as a riverboat was named after him and the Merseys perform two songs about that boat - the very popular 'Waiting For The Robert E. Lee' and the lesser known 'Sailing On The Robert E. Lee'.

New Orleans music historian, **Connie Atkinson (1)**: "Music was very much a part of city life. There were so many different languages that they couldn't understand each other, so dancing seemed like a good idea. Even when the city only had 10,000 people, it had several dance halls and a full-time opera house. So many different kinds of music were played in New Orleans and so many different kinds of people came there and brought their own traditions with them. New Orleans was very open to music and entertainment - everybody got along so long as everybody wanted to party - and jazz came out of that. Louis Armstrong was around in the heyday when it all came together and he proved to be a great ambassador for the city."

The song 'Way Down Yonder In New Orleans' describes it as "Heaven right here on earth", but it was paradise with a stench as it didn't have any organised disposal for sewage until 1892. The sewage problems might explain Louis Armstrong's lifelong obsession with his bowels. Disease was rife and infant mortality, in particular, was very high.

As the emancipated slaves struggled to survive, music gave them comfort and as the majority could not read or write, it was their only form of cultural entertainment. The music that the Africans knew were the drumming and chants from back home. They did not know European instruments like trumpets and trombones, which had been imported into America. Both sides in the Civil War had marching bands and marching tunes ('Marching Through Georgia', 'The Battle Hymn Of The Republic') and once the war was over, the instruments became obsolete. They could be bought cheaply in pawn shops and gradually, the black musicians learnt to play them. They knew nothing of key changes and could not read music, so they were learning by experimentation. The way the African-Americans adapted their heritage led to the creation of jazz, and their descendants became a major force in American popular culture.

Tony Davis (2): "Jazz music is black American folk music, derived from the blues and gospel and spirituals, and it is a vocal music. Before people had any instruments, the black people in New Orleans and places like that would sing these songs and when they were finally able to buy instruments - the brass bands disbanded after the Civil War and they were able to buy instruments in the pawn shops - they didn't know anything about technique so they played them in a vocal way. That's where traditional jazz comes from. It's a simplification but the trumpet is the tenor singing, the clarinet represents the women's voices weaving around it, and the trombones are the baritones down below doing the harmonies."

II

The first inklings of jazz were heard in the marching bands in New Orleans in the 1890s. The bands featured brass instruments and drums and would play the popular songs of the day at parties and carnivals or more appropriate ones for weddings and funerals. It's not practicable to play short tunes while marching so the melodies would be played in extended versions. To alleviate boredom, the more capable musicians began to improvise. These variations indicate the beginnings of jazz, which led to the formation of Buddy

Bolden's band in 1895. The word 'jass', later 'jazz', probably comes from the initials of the marching hymn, 'Jesus Almighty, Save our Souls'.

Connie Atkinson (3): "Anybody who has seen 'Live And Let Die' will know what a New Orleans funeral is like. Jazz funerals aren't for everyone and they are usually for what Mahalia Jackson called 'sportin' men'. On the way to the funeral, sad songs would be played by a brass band but on the way back, you cut the body loose and you play joyous songs, which is very much an African tradition."

Ken Baldwin (4): "Many jazz fans overlook the importance of the banjo as the instrument has become the butt of jokes. The jazz bands from the early part of the century would all include banjos. You couldn't trundle along with a piano when you were marching through the streets of New Orleans. The banjo was the only instrument carrying the chord sequences of the tunes and it was louder than a guitar. I like the banjo very much and there are some numbers where I wouldn't dream of using my guitar."

The first musicians had menial jobs and few worked as professional or even semi-professional musicians. Playing music was their hobby and there was a sense of fulfilment about what they were doing. The music was happy and uplifting and 'When The Saints Go Marching In', which was written in 1896, is a fine example. As is evident from the title, it is also a marching tune.

Charles 'Buddy' Bolden, who was born in 1877, became a leading cornet player in New Orleans and when he played the low notes on his 1904 composition 'Funky Butt', women would scream in ecstasy. The title meant 'black bottom' and today 'funky music' is still primarily black and 'butt' has come back into use for a backside. Bolden had a residency at the Funky Butt dance hall, but he was an alcoholic and was committed to an insane asylum in 1906. He never recovered and although he died in obscurity in 1931, he is remembered by the jazz standard, 'I Thought I Heard Buddy Bolden Say' and through a new Funky Butt ballroom in New Orleans.

In 1897 the alderman Joseph Story sponsored legislation that would confine prostitution to a single area, which became known as Storyville. In actuality, there were two areas - one for white and one for black prostitutes. The mixed race Creoles, who had often come from the Caribbean, were in the black sector as a law passed in 1894 stated that anyone of mixed blood would be considered black.

Many reference books link the origins of jazz to these brothels, but is that likely? Would a brothel be big enough to support its own entertainment and, in any event, would the clientèle be interested? I would have thought that most men would have gone to a brothel, done the business and gone home. Maybe visiting a prostitute was more of a social event than it is today, but I doubt it. There may have been piano rolls (in which the notes are reproduced on perforated, thick paper and played back on a pseudo-piano) or a live pianist at the larger establishments to entertain you while you waited your turn, but not much more. In 1917 the US Navy put Storyville out of bounds because the sailors were always brawling or contracting VD there. According to many sources, the musicians moved to Chicago and Kansas City when Storyville was closed, but again I can't see a mass exodus - and did they take the girls with them? All rubbish.

Derek Vaux (5): "I have a good friend, Art Varvoutis, who lives in up state Louisiana at Covington. He took me on my first and only visit to New Orleans. This entailed driving across a dead-straight 26 mile long causeway across Lake Ponchartrain to the north of New Orleans. It was like driving out to sea and as the weather was very humid, we soon lost sight of land. Then eventually what appeared to be a distant cloud formation slowly materialised into a vast city with huge skyscrapers looming out of the haze on the horizon. It was a deeply emotional and eerie way to approach the home of jazz. After what Art called his Acme Auto Tour of the city, we finished up in the French Quarter. It was desperately hot and sticky, but I was there at last, standing in Storyville - 'The District'. With my hands across the bridge of my nose and looking upwards, it was exactly the same as I imagined it must have been 100 years ago with the fabulous architecture all there to be seen, savoured and appreciated, but with my hands raised a few more inches and looking around at eye-level, the view was horrendous. Hordes of tourists, beggars, hookers, vulgar T-shirts and fast food stores interspersed with countless bars, most of which were advertising 'live jazz', but in every case were presenting some ghastly form of rock music. The only place completely untouched by time was Preservation Hall, but standing in the courtyard alongside the hall and hearing the appallingly played jazz that was emanating from this historic structure, I wanted out. My host eagerly enquired if I'd had enough - he'd seen it before and far too many times for his own liking - and when I dumbly nodded, I was back in the air-conditioned comfort of his car and back across the Pontchartrain Bridge before I could moan 'Buddy Bolden'. I'd been there and seen where it all happened, but I'll never go back."

III

One of the delights of a jazz festival today is an umbrella parade. **Frank Robinson (6)**: "The umbrella parade goes back to the marching bands in New Orleans before the First World War. The front line has at least one umbrella at the front and it would be followed by people dancing to the rhythm of the street parade. Terry Birkinhead is an expert at it, he is rhythmical and loosely-jointed and is wonderful at getting all the women to follow him. We play 'Bourbon Street Parade' or 'Cake Walking Babies (From Home)', nothing too fast."

Terry Birkinhead (7): "I don't play an instrument but I've been very keen on jazz since my teens. In the early 1990s I led a couple of parades for fun, and then Tommy Orrit from the Savoy Jazzmen died and I was asked if I would do something for his funeral at Springwood Cemetery. I got a black frock coat, bowler hat and sash and I was very nervous as I knew Tom very well and I wanted to do justice to his memory. 26 Merseyside musicians were involved and it was very moving. I have done about 20 jazz funerals and 25 parades by now and it is always a privilege to lead the band. I find the parades very exciting and it's like leading a conga. There are no set steps but a good sense of rhythm is essential. It was wonderful to do one to promote the Hamilton Quarter Jazz Festival. Jazz people knew what it was all about but the general public had never seen anything like it. Many people make their own brollies and take a pride in having something different."

Tony Davis (8): "The umbrellas are what the ladies had at picnics and funerals in New Orleans and they would dress with the parasols and dance behind the marching bands. We have the Wirral Jazz Marching Band every year for the Hoylake Lifeboats and Terry Birkinhead does his dance in front with his special umbrella, but they do it at jazz festivals now and the ladies vie with each other for the best-decorated umbrellas. It gets people involved, if you're not a musician, you can get an umbrella and prance about."

Terry Birkinhead (9): "For the funerals, I have a special purple and gold brolly - it has 'Walking with the King' on one side and 'Over in the Gloryland' on the other. The band usually plays the coffin out of the house to the hearse and if it is a short distance, we have also led the funeral procession to the church. It is always a dirge, a slow march, up to the committal and after that the soul has gone to heaven, so there are no mourners on this earth and it is all joy. The band can let loose and play some bright music. It becomes a happy occasion and people are dancing. We do it wrong to some extent because at the New Orleans funerals, the band only went as far as the cemetery gates. They would wait for them to come out and then march them back home. I've done some funerals where, at a respectful distance from the graveside, the band plays a slow tune and then they might go into 'When The Saints Go Marching In'."

IV

The darker side of jazz is represented by the blues, although that is by no means as bleak as it is often depicted. The blues is a musical form in its own right and was often performed by solo performers. Such famed performers as Huddie Ledbetter (Leadbelly) and Blind Lemon Jefferson were singing publicly as early as 1905. One of the earliest blues is 'Snag It' but no one knows what snagging refers to now. Considering the sexual playfulness of so many of the blues, this might be just as well.

The standard format is a 12-bar blues and each verse usually consists of three lines. The first two lines are identical and describe a situation and the third comments upon it. When Paul Jones performs his tribute to Sonny Boy Williamson, he prefaces it by telling of the difficulties when the Manfred Mann band backed him in the 1960s: he says, "Naively, we thought there were 12 bars in a 12-bar blues."

W.C. Handy, the son of a preacher man , was born in 1873 and became a composer, bandleader and cornet player. A statue in Memphis proclaims him as 'The Father Of The Blues'. A sophisticated man, he heard Mississippi street singers performing the blues and he took snatches of their words and melodies as a base for his own compositions. In 1903 W.C. Handy heard a guitarist at a railway station whining a song about 'de yeller dawg', the area being serviced by the Yellow Dog trains, the colloquial name for the Yazoo Delta Railroad. The fragment stayed with him and some years later he wrote 'Yellow Dog Rag', which was subsequently renamed 'Yellow Dog Blues'.

When Handy was in Chicago in 1920, he heard a woman hanging clothes out to dry and singing, 'Your clothes looks lonesome, hanging on the line'. Again, knowing a good idea when he heard one, he continued to Brownlee's Barber Shop and wrote 'Aunt Hagar's Blues' while he was waiting. It was performed that very night by Erskine Tate's Orchestra in the Vendome Theatre. Other writers copied Handy's approach and, in 1915, this led to two blues, Handy's 'Hesitating Blues' and 'Hesitation Blues', being based upon the same hymn. Another of Handy's blues, 'Careless Love', was written in 1921, but doubtless he heard somebody singing something first.

Naturally, these itinerant singers did not share any composing credits or royalties. However, in 1912 Handy himself was furious when he was cheated out of his royalties on 'The Memphis Blues', which was written for Ed Crump as his campaign song for mayor of Memphis. Handy did not make the same mistake with his most famous composition, 'St Louis Blues', which was written in 1914. The song became so famous that it was used as the title for a 1958 film biography of his life starring Nat 'King' Cole.

V

A dance called the Cake Walk had been imported from the Caribbean and although the Merseysippi Jazz Band still play Cake

Walks - 'Smokey Mokes' and 'Cake Walking Babies (From Home)' - nobody today would know the correct dance steps. The Cake Walk developed into a piano-based, bouncy music known as Ragtime. Ragtime used missed beats to great effect and it was named when a patron called out, "Play that ragged music again." Ragtime had a syncopated beat played with the pianist's left hand while the melody and the ragged time flowed from the right.

The pianist Scott Joplin, who was born in Texarkana, Texas, in 1868 heard ragtime music while he was living in Sedalia, Missouri. The better pianists went to the Maple Leaf Club and Joplin immortalised the club in his 1899 composition, 'Maple Leaf Rag'. A white music publisher, John Stark, loved the tune and its success locally and then nationally enabled the 60 year old Stark to move to St Louis and set up a considerable publishing empire. Much to his credit, Stark did not cheat Joplin and he became a rich man through such compositions as 'Original Rags' (1899), 'The Entertainer' (1902), 'Gladiolus Rag' (1907) and 'Fig Leaf Rag' (1908). Joplin would write on the sheet music, "Do not play this piece fast. It is never right to play ragtime fast."

Joplin lost his audience by making his rags too complicated and by writing a ballet and two operas that did not find a following. Indeed, the loss of a baby daughter and then the failure of the opera, 'Treemonisha', in 1911 destroyed his spirit and he is said to have died a broken man in 1917. Maybe, but the cause of his death was syphilis. I have a 1970 LP of his piano rags played by Joshua Rifkin and Rifkin writes in the notes, "The awakening of interest in black culture and history during the last decade has not yet resurrected Joplin." In 1973 Paul Newman and Robert Redford starred in 'The Sting' and changed that.

In 1910 Irving Berlin, a Jewish songwriter from a New York ghetto, wrote 'Alexander's Ragtime Band'. Despite the title, the song is more of a march and lacks the syncopation of ragtime. It was included in an unsuccessful Broadway revue, 'The Happy Whirl', but it was so cheerful that it was soon picked up by other performers. A million copies of its sheet music were sold in a year and just as UK citizens purchased televisions to see the Coronation, many Americans bought the new-fangled record-players to play 'Alexander's Ragtime Band', which is associated with Al Jolson. This invention, together with the radio and cinema, was to speed up the acceptance of American music, both black and white, and also lead to its popularity in Europe.

The first jazz record 'The Original Dixieland One Step' / 'Livery Stable Blues', was by a white ensemble from New Orleans, the Original Dixieland Jass Band (note the original spelling) in 1917. It did well and the next year they sold a million copies of 'Tiger Rag'. Their other successes include 'Indiana', 'Jazz Me Blues', 'Ostrich Walk', 'Clarinet Marmalade' and 'At The Jazz Band Ball'.

In New Orleans, a Creole pianist, Ferdinand Joseph Lemott, who was born in 1890, began playing the piano in Storyville clubs when he was only 12 years old. His parents disapproved but he took little notice and soon he had merged blues and ragtime with Latin music to create his own musical gumbo. He was very proud of his European heritage and sometimes passed himself off as a Spaniard to avoid problems from the Ku Klux Klan. Ferdinand adopted the colourful pseudonym of Jelly Roll Morton.

George Melly (10): "A jelly roll was a black synonym for the male organ. It was a cake like a swiss roll but with jelly replacing jam, so it is a simple case of phallic symbolism. The black audiences knew very well what a jelly roll was, but the white powers of the day probably didn't. There were songs like 'I Ain't Gonna Give Nobody None O' This Jelly Roll' and Bessie Smith sang 'Nobody in town can bake a good jelly roll like mine'. I love performing risque songs myself, songs like 'Nuts' and 'I Like My Fanny Brown'. I find them amusing and ribald and certainly the people who come to my concerts are not the sort of people who are going to be offended by sexual innuendo."

Although Jelly Roll Morton claimed to have invented jazz, this is fantasy. He was, however, one of its first composers, copyrighting 'Original Jelly Roll Blues' and 'Wolverine Blues' in 1915. Many of his tunes are still played today including 'Shreveport Stomp', 'Sidewalk Blues' and 'The Chant', which was originally called 'Spooky Serenade'. 'Big Fat Ham' is also known as 'Ham And Eggs' and 'Big Foot Ham', which makes no sense: is 'Big Foot Ham' due to Jelly Roll's bad writing?

Jelly Roll Morton created such a full sound as a solo pianist that it sounds like more than one instrument on his early records. His classic recordings are with the Red Hot Peppers between 1926 and 1928, but his career was in decline by 1930. He wrote a poignant comment on how he felt the world was treating him, 'If Someone Would Only Love Me', but his composition 'King Porter Stomp' became a hit for Benny Goodman during the Swing era in 1935. Still, no one paid much attention to Jelly Roll Morton himself and he died in 1941, ironically when a revival of New Orleans music was taking place.

Monty Sunshine (11): "I love New Orleans jazz, it is absolutely lovely music. I can still learn a lot from listening to King Oliver and Louis Armstrong and one of my all-times favourites is 'Mournful Serenade' by Jelly Roll Morton."

George Melly (12): "One of my favourite songs is one that Jelly Roll Morton never recorded with words during his career but he did sing it at the piano when he was telling his life story in the Library of Congress to Alan Lomax. It is called 'Sweet Substitute' and it has all the qualities I admire in Morton's compositions, that tough tenderness. John Chilton realised that Flanagan and Allen's 'Home Town', which they sing in a very cheerful way, had that same sweet and sour melancholy and we treat it like a Morton number."

John Chilton (13): "I came in from school one day and switched on the radio and heard a Jelly Roll Morton record, 'I Thought I Heard Buddy Bolden Say'. I was hooked from that moment on, I thought this was the music for me and I could find no one in my village in Northamptonshire who knew anything about jazz. I went into town and bought a record catalogue and tried to work out who I wanted to hear, and that set me on the path of jazz research. There's a magic to jazz. Once you're hooked, you learn more about the music and the things that sounded good years ago still sound good."

VI

The 1920s, the so-called Jazz Age, was an extraordinary decade in popular music and also led to a greater relaxation in social attitudes. Because of the new means of mass communication, artists could become national, and even international, stars. In 1920 the composer John Philip Sousa objected to 'canned music' on the radio. Dances like the Charleston and the fox-trot quickly gained acceptance. The tune, 'Bee's Knees', was a tribute to Bee Jackson, a champion charleston dancer, and the phrase is used to describe excellence today. The microphone enabled singers to perform much more intimately and the first performer to benefit from this was Bing Crosby, who sang with Paul Whiteman's orchestra.

Al Jolson was the principal performer of 'Alexander's Ragtime Band' and introduced numerous hit songs - 'Swanee', 'You Made Me Love You' and 'California Here I Come' among them. Although the minstrel days of blackface performers were drawing to an end, Al Jolson started using make up because his Negro dresser had told him, "You'd be much funnier, boss, if you blacked your face like mine. People always laugh at the black man." At the time, nobody thought this was offensive - or, indeed, years later when George Mitchell revived the concept for 'The Black And Minstrel Show' on stage and TV.

John Chilton (14): "People don't like the black tradition of comedy now as it is considered racist but in the early days it was the way of black people entertaining black people. They loved it and when it was parodied by white people with hideous make-up and grotesque actions, it became a symbol of people trying to make fun and so take advantage of black people. The actual black minstrelsy is an old tradition and a noble one in that it allowed great artists to emerge, who were featured in films and on records like Louis Jordan."

The first talking film was the musical 'The Jazz Singer' starring Al Jolson in 1927, which put many silent movie pianists out of work, but established Jolson as "the world's greatest entertainer". Jolson only sang five songs in the film, but 'Toot, Toot, Tootsie', 'Blue Skies' and 'My Mammy' were among them. Sociologically, the film is intriguing as Jolson deals with issues surrounding being a first-generation Jew in America. 'The Jazz Singer' contrasts the sacred with the profane, black with white and the Jew with the Gentile (including Jolson's love for a shiksa). Bobby Gordon who played the young Jolson (or rather the young Jakie Rabinowitz) sang

20

"Waiting For The Robert E. Lee'. He is criticised by his father, a cantor, for singing "nigger songs in a beer garden".

VII

In 'Animal Farm', some animals were more equal than others. In jazz ensembles, it was usually the trumpet or cornet player who stood out. Speaking very generally, the trumpet or cornet player stays with the melody or doesn't stray too far. The trombonist plays the harmonies and the clarinet player provides the counter-harmonies.

For a few years, Buddy Bolden was the leading musician in New Orleans, but then the interest passed to Joe Oliver, who was dubbed 'King' by his trombonist Kid Ory, although he was, in turn, surpassed by his young protégé, Louis Armstrong.

Louis Armstrong, born on 4 August 1901, was the son of a prostitute who did her best to raise him in a crime-ridden district. When he was only 12, Armstrong was jailed for firing a gun. He might have become another sorry statistic, but music was his salvation. King Oliver recognised his musical talent and, when Oliver moved to Chicago in 1918, he recommended that the young Louis should take his place. Four years later he sent for him and thus established King Oliver's Creole Jazz Band with its unique two cornets lead. They played at the Plantation, an opulent club financed with Mafia money. This was common in Chicago: Earl Hines played the Grand Terrace for ten years not because he liked the club so much but because the owner would shoot him if he left. Was Chicago called a toddling town because of what might happen to your knees if you stepped out of line? Also, many people in New Orleans were ambivalent towards Louis Armstrong because he left the city, a feeling akin to that in Liverpool for the Beatles.

In 2000 **Robin Tankard (15)** made a CD, 'Liverpool Steamer', as part of the Merseyside ensemble, Roy Potts' Five And A Penny Jazz Band: "The photograph on the front of the CD is the Natchez, which is one of the old riverboats that used to take Louis Armstrong to Chicago. We were lucky enough to play on it when we did a jazz tour with the Dukes of Dixieland."

21

Roy Potts (16): "There has to be a big Louis Armstrong influence for every trumpet player, who plays jazz music. 'The Stage' called me a Louis Armstrong lookalike, which I can't believe, as we're different colours."

Humphrey Lyttelton (17): "Anyone who ever played jazz on any instrument at any stage in the game has had some influence from Louis Armstrong. Certainly piano players, and even if you play double-bass. He is one of the great influences on jazz music: Charlie Parker had a similar effect on modern jazz. He was a big influence on me both as a trumpet player and as a musician, but since then I have taken on more influences. From the point of view of learning how to get the best out of a seven piece band, my big influence is Duke Ellington."

Jazz history was made with the first recording session by King Oliver's Creole Jazz Band in Richmond, Indiana in April 1923. Nine titles were recorded in a single day including 'Dippermouth Blues', 'Chimes Blues', 'Mandy Lee Blues', 'Snake Rag','Weather Bird Rag' and 'I'm Going Away To Wear You Off My Mind'. The technical quality of the recordings is far from perfect, but the music is essential, some of the finest jazz ever recorded. It is not, however, a showcase for Armstrong as several of the players are allowed to shine.

John Lawrence (18): "Louis Armstrong started playing as a very young man, fully formed: the first records he ever made are wonderful and they still are wonderful today. I'm sure he knew right from the start how good he was."

Kenny Ball (19): "You can play all of Louis' notes close to his timing but you can never get the same tone. Some guys get very close but you can always tell an imitator as the tone eludes them. I don't know how he did it but he was incredible. He never played too loud and yet he always sounded so powerful."

Humphrey Lyttelton (20): "The first band that famously used two trumpets was in 1923. King Oliver was the leader and he was with the young Louis Armstrong. The tradition for two trumpets or trumpet and cornet or two cornets was recharged in the 1940s when Lu Watters and the Yerba Buena band started up in San

Francisco and they used two cornets operating in harmony. The King Oliver band was much looser with Armstrong playing an independent second part. It is a time-honoured thing and when it is done properly, as the Merseys do, it is an exciting sound."

The Merseysippi Jazz Band have a novel arrangement of 'Chimes Blues', reworking the piano section on King Oliver's version. **John Lawrence (21)** comments, "The front line takes turns to play one note each in 'Chimes Blues' and so there are 72 opportunities to play a wrong note."

Robin Tankard (22): "I was 16 years old when the Kid Ory band came to the Liverpool Empire. I had just taken up the bass and I asked this nice little old man, 'Excuse me, sir, how do you do that thing with the bass?' He grabbed my hand and said 'You do it like this' and nearly broke my wrist. I said, 'Did you know Louis Armstrong?' He said, 'I was with the King Oliver Band when Louis was a young boy in short pants who came and played with us.'"

A few months after those first recordings, King Oliver's Creole Jazz Band was back in the studio with 'Where Did You Stay Last Night' (written by Louis and his wife, Lil, who knew he had a roving eye), 'Chattanooga Stomp', 'Working Man Blues', 'Someday Sweetheart' and 'Mabel's Dream'. Despite playing in such a creative environment, Armstrong left Oliver in 1924 as his wife, Lil, convinced him that he needed more money and he needed to grow. He moved to another Mafia stronghold, New York, to join Fletcher Henderson.

In New York in October 1924 Armstrong recorded 'Copenhagen' with Fletcher Henderson and his Orchestra and a few days later, 'Of All The Wrongs You've Done To Me' with Clarence Williams' Blue Five. This record was marred by a vocal from Clarence Williams' wife, Eva Taylor. In 1927 Clarence wrote a musical, 'Bottomland', for his wife and the MJB has recorded a song from that musical, 'I'm Going Back To Bottomland'.

In December 1924 Louis recorded 'Mandy, Make Up Your Mind' with Fletcher Henderson and his Orchestra and a few days later repeated the song for Clarence Williams' Blue Five. At that session he also recorded 'I'm A Little Blackbird Looking For A Bluebird'. A couple of days after that Louis was part of the Red Onion Jazz Babies recording 'Cake Walking Babies (From Home)', which he then recorded with Clarence Williams' Blue Five. Recording was so new that nobody had given any thoughts to exclusivity contracts.

As an example of the nonchalant way the sessions took place, a band called the New Orleans Wanderers made some recordings on 13 July 1926. The next day they returned to the studios as the New Orleans Bootblacks. Had they all found jobs overnight? One of the recordings from the second day, 'Flat Foot', is in the Merseys' repertoire.

Also in 1924, Louis accompanied Ma Rainey on 'See See Rider' and 'Jelly Bean Blues'. In 1925 he did the same for Bessie Smith on some legendary recordings including 'St Louis Blues', 'Careless Love Blues' and 'You've Been A Good Old Wagon'. Bessie Smith also recorded 'Muddy Water' without Armstrong's involvement.

George Melly (23): "A lot of these scratchy old records have been cleaned up with immense care and patience and they sound so good on the CD reissues. In any event, I feel that people should be getting under the surface of those scratchy old records and listening to the genius. Bessie Smith is my great heroine - everything she did is so beautiful and I would choose 'Young Woman's Blues' as my favourite. I love 'You've Been A Good Old Wagon'. People think that feminism only happened yesterday afternoon but that song and several others prove that, in blues circles at any rate, it was around in the 1920s. A lot of the blues singers didn't stick to the blues and they sang the popular songs of the day. Bessie Smith sang 'Alexander's Ragtime Band' and it's more the spirit of the blues that they dealt with. I like that approach as I would find a double CD of T-Bone Walker singing the blues rather monotonous. On the whole, I prefer black singers to white, but there are exceptions and Jimmie Rodgers was a remarkable singer."

John Lawrence (24): "You can take almost any tune that has ever been written and give it a jazz flavour. Jazz is not a type of music, it is an approach to music. For example, Tommy Dorsey's 'Song Of India' is a long way from its classical origins."

Chris Barber (25): "It isn't right to say that you have to have lived the blues to sing them. You might say just as well that you have got to have a religious experience to sing 'Ave Maria'. Bessie Smith was never flooded out of her home and yet she sang 'Muddy Water'. You have to be able to understand human feelings and to be able to express them in a sympathetic way. None of the blues singers I knew had been in jail and yet they sang about it. The prison population of the States was 10% black and 90% white and so whites were on the chain gangs too."

John Lawrence (26): "In his younger days, George Melly used to say that it was a little embarrassing for a young white man to try and sound like a middle-aged black woman, but he found he couldn't sing the songs with an English accent. You have to go some way towards singing it their way, and that has been very successful for him."

In 1925 Louis Armstrong recorded 'King Porter Stomp' with Fletcher Henderson and his Orchestra. Forming his own Hot Five with Kid Ory on trombone towards the end of that year, the band recorded 'My Heart'. Armstrong was soon adding his gruff vocals which sounded great but contrasted with the trained voices normally heard on records. In 1926, when singing 'Heebie Jeebies', he dropped the lyric sheet and improvised some nonsense. This is the start of scat singing. A few minutes later, he recorded two more legendary tracks, 'Cornet Chop Suey' and 'Muskrat Ramble'.

John Lawrence (27) says, "'Cornet Chop Suey' is a tour de force by Louis Armstrong and we turned it into a two horn version on the grounds that if we couldn't outplay Louis, we could at least outnumber him."

Acker Bilk (28): "Louis' version of 'Muskrat Ramble' with Kid Ory on trombone and Johnny Dodds on clarinet always knocks me out. I like all his old stuff and in fact, I like everything as even 'What A Wonderful World' shows what a good singer he is. His timing is unbelievable and his voice was so infectious and unusual. 'Blueberry Hill' is marvellous. If he hadn't played trumpet the way he did, he would have made it as a singer."

In 1926 Armstrong recorded 'Sunset Café Stomp', named after a favourite haunt in Chicago. In 1927 he guested with Johnny Dodds' Black Bottom Stompers (the name coming from a popular dance that for a short while rivalled the Charleston in popularity) for 'Weary Blues'. As this is a relatively simple tune, the Merseys have combined it with 'Farewell Blues'.

One of Armstrong's most celebrated recordings is 'Potato Head Blues' from 1927. Armstrong plays the melody in a standard fashion at first but then improvises around the chord changes. Unlike today's recording sessions, there are no early takes to determine how the performer came by such invention. As Armstrong also wrote the melody, it would be good to know what his original intentions were.

The following day he cut 'Melancholy Blues'. A few months later, Kid Ory was given a chance to shine on 'Ory's Creole Trombone', the Everest for jazz trombonists. With his Hot Five, Louis also recorded 'Once In A While', which has become as popular as 'The Saints' in the Merseys' repertoire. One of Armstrong's last recordings on the cornet was 'Savoy Blues' in 1927. This simple blues riff has Kid Ory as the writer - as if...

John Higham (29): "Louis is so good that you can't imitate him. We do set pieces like 'Potato Head Blues' for two trumpets, but you can't ever approach the freshness with which he played, so he is an enormous inspiration."

Les Harris (30): "Louis was a wonderful trumpet player, one note and it's instant recognition. It may take a bar or two to recognise other trumpet players but not Louis. It's tone and texture, the whole thing, the whole feeling. It is incredible to be able to do that."

John Higham (31): "A good trumpeter should have a distinctive voice, and you can recognise Louis a mile off. One note and I know it's him. His tone was so wide in the low register and it stayed wide all the way up to the top. A lot of modern players will go high but it is a thin tone by the time they get up there. The way Louis managed it was incredible."

Kenny Ball (32): "Louis Armstrong said that if you have to ask about playing jazz, then you'll never know. You need to have some aptitude but you've either got swing or you haven't. I don't think I swung very much at first, but I never cease to marvel at what I can do on the trumpet. When I'm relaxed and playing well, I sometimes amaze myself with what I'm doing. A band still sounds like a band if it's got arrangements, but if it's on good form and swinging, you can extend the solos and sound really good. Duke Ellington summed it up with 'It Don't Mean A Thing If It Ain't Got That Swing'."

Humphrey Lyttelton (33): "The great thing about jazz is that it's not a style or a way of playing, but a characteristic and a voice. Everybody wants an individual sound. It is not just Louis Armstrong. With all the well-known jazz musicians, I can tell within a bar or two who it is."

By 1928 Louis Armstrong had permanently switched from cornet to trumpet.

John Lawrence (34): "A cornet is a smaller instrument and has a more mellow tone. A trumpet has a bit more brilliance, tonally speaking, but there is not a great deal of difference. The cornet is used more in silver and military bands, while the trumpet is used more in orchestral settings. I have always played the cornet, simply because it is more comfortable to play. It's like choosing a putter when you're playing golf: if it suits you, you stick to it."

In 1928 Louis made his famed recordings of 'Basin Street Blues' and 'West End Blues' (with its wonderful unaccompanied start) and he also accompanied Lillie Delk Christian on 'Sweethearts On Parade', which he recorded in his own right in 1930. Louis, who smoked marijuana every day of his working life, recorded his paean to the drug, 'Muggles', in 1928. Starting with 'Ain't Misbehavin'' in 1929, Louis Armstrong - he pronounced his name 'Lewis' - also performed the popular songs of the day. He recorded ' I Can't Believe That You're In Love With Me' and 'You're Driving Me Crazy' in 1930. In 1931 he was the first to record the standard 'Lazy River'. Sadly, King Oliver's popularity was fading as quickly as Armstrong's was rising. Oliver did write 'Sweet Like This' which he recorded in 1929, but by then no one was paying much attention.

Humphrey Lyttelton (35): "The first Louis Armstrong record I heard was 'Basin Street Blues'. It was a tour de force - it bowled me over and it has remained a favourite of mine ever since. I don't think he took his singing very seriously at first - he had an extrovert, bawling style, but when Bing Crosby came along, he started softening his voice and singing the popular songs of the day. It was still a gravel voice but he found he could phrase in a very passionate and rhapsodic way, especially on slow ballads."

Kenny Ball (36): "Louis swung like the clappers on just about everything he recorded. He recorded some crap in his time but he was always able to make a silk purse out of a sow's ear. I love 'West End Blues', which is very hard to play even for modern trumpet players. He plays one high note, a top B flat, and he puts more feeling into that note that some guys could put into a thousand. It's not just the technique but the emotional content he puts into it. He used to sing in the same way, but it's pretty obvious from the way he sung the songs that the original lyrics weren't written in stone. I even like 'What A Wonderful World': it sounds flowery and sentimental, but it makes the point that there is more good than bad in the world, and that's how I look at life myself."

Much as I love his music, I am always uncomfortable when I see footage of Louis Armstrong. He is a brilliant, mesmerising performer but there seems to be a strong Uncle Tom element with his continuous mugging. Until the end of the 60s, many black performers presented a cheerful personality to the public who might otherwise feel threatened. You can see this most distinctly in the careful grooming of Tamla-Motown performers and how Marvin Gaye, in the wake of black consciousness, publicly became a much more troubled and complex personality. Maybe that's just the way Louis was, but no serious black performer starting today would appear like that.

John Higham (37): "I don't think he was Uncle Tomming, but he thought of himself more as an entertainer than a jazz musician. If he found that something worked by wriggling his chops around or by rolling his eyes, he would keep doing it. He was playing a concert once for only 40 people and he was playing exactly as he did for 10,000. The trombone player said, 'Louis, don't knock yourself out. There's hardly anyone here' and he said, 'One of those people might have driven 400 miles to see me.' That was very perceptive of him."

VIII

The main contender for Armstrong's crown for the jazz musician of the 20th century is Duke Ellington. He was born in Washington in 1899 and he played piano, studied harmony and wrote his first songs while still in his teens. He moved to New York in 1923 and formed his own band the following year. By 1927 the band had secured a residency at the Cotton Club, a recording contract and regular radio broadcasts. He wrote both 'Black And Tan Fantasy' and 'Creole Love Call' in 1927 and his famed 'Mood Indigo' in 1930. He maintained a highly talented orchestra who were able to meet his challenges and innovative arrangements and some of them - Harry Carney, Billy Strayhorn, Cootie Williams - are legendary in their own right. Ellington's standards include 'Sophisticated Lady', 'It Don't Mean A Thing If It Ain't Got That Swing', 'Prelude To A Kiss', 'Don't Get Around Much Anymore' and 'I'm Beginning To See The Light'.

Duke Ellington's interests proved to be as wide as George Gershwin's and he wrote suites, concertos and experimental pieces. The MJB has a great love of his work and have recorded several of his tunes including 'Saturday Night Function' and 'Misty Morning'. He must have liked 'East St Louis Toodle-oo' himself as he recorded it 12 times between 1926 and 1937. 'Sweet Mama' from 1929 was even neglected by Ellington as he later wrote another tune with the same title.

John Higham (38): "I love doing growl trumpet work so Bubber Miley from the Duke Ellington's orchestra and Cootie Williams inspire me. They had this growl sound in the late 20s, which is quite exciting to produce if you get it right."

A Liverpool jazz musician from the 1950s, **Noel Walker (39)**, became a record producer and, much to his surprise, found himself producing Duke Ellington in 1969: "It was a great, great pleasure to be asked to record Duke Ellington for his 70th birthday concert and it was going right back to my jazz roots. The impresario Robert Patterson asked United Artists to do it and because of my

29

background, they thought that I was the right man for the job. The band was warming up when I got to the theatre and they sounded horrible and sad and floppy. Duke was very tired at the time but as soon as the announcer said, 'Ladies and gentlemen, Duke Ellington', the whole band sat up and Duke roared. Cat Anderson blew his balls off with 'Rockin' In Rhythm'. That is one of the most exciting tracks I have heard and there's another great track on there, '4.30 Blues'. The band was tired and shattered but they picked themselves up by their bootstrings to produce those performances. The LP worked out wonderfully and I was asked to make Duke's next album as well. Duke sent me a Christmas card with kisses every year because it was such a good album and the best-selling album he'd had in 20 years." Noel Walker produced his second live album for Duke Ellington in 1971 and they have been packaged as 'The English Concerts, 1969 and 1971' on Sequel NED CD 183.

IX

A white musician Bix Beiderbecke was born into a middle-class family in Iowa in 1903. He was impressed by the records of the Original Dixieland Jazz Band and, much to his parents' disapproval, decided to play the music himself. He played the cornet with Paul Whiteman's Orchestra and worked with other musicians on sessions. He recorded both 'Singin' The Blues', which he wrote, and 'I'm Coming Virginia' in 1927. Once on a visit home, he discovered the records that he had sent to his parents in a cupboard and still in their wrapping paper. Maybe that contributed to his drinking as after a few years of erratic performances, Beiderbecke died of alcoholism in 1931, although it may have been the homemade liquor of the Prohibition era that finished him off. He is viewed as a martyr to his music and a novel by Dorothy Baker, 'Young Man With A Horn', romanticised his life. He is one of the first musicians to embody "cool", a term also used to describe Chet Baker and Miles Davis.

Kenny Baker (40): "Louis was a Negro trumpet player with a dark sound. Bix and also Red Nichols had a white sound, which was a different approach entirely. Everything Bix played was pure and clean and so beautifully melodic. He did some marvellous things with Paul Whiteman, but unfortunately he drank too much and didn't look after himself."

John Higham (41): "If you look at the repertoire of Jelly Roll Morton, Louis Armstrong and Bix Beiderbecke, you will find that they played some wonderful tunes which I never tire of playing. I do admit that they didn't always have good taste. Bix recorded 'Barnacle Bill The Sailor' and Wild Bill Davison's first professional recording was 'Horsey, Keep Your Tail Up'."

Kenny Ball (42): "All Bix's recordings are favourites of mine - I love 'Singin' The Blues' and 'Ostrich Walk'. He didn't have a legitimate technique. He picked up the cornet and found out what notes made what sound. He never used the correct technique of playing the first and second valve and he used the third valve instead."

X

The Harlem pianist Fats Waller recorded any number of cheerful love songs. He wrote 'Ain't Misbehavin'' and 'Honeysuckle Rose' and coming from a religious home, he was often in turmoil about whether he should be performing in night clubs. Not that it stopped him consuming the goods: he could eat 20 pork chops and drink a bottle of gin at a single sitting, and he had the figure to prove it. In 1931 he recorded 'I'm Crazy 'Bout My Baby' and, in 1932, W.C. Handy's 'Yellow Dog Blues'. In 1934 he wrote 'How Can You Face Me?' for the Muzak Company. In 1935 he recorded five songs in one session in New York City. Before he left, a recording executive begged him to record a new song. Fats played it through, quickly assigned parts to his musicians, and 'I'm Gonna Sit Right Down And Write Myself A Letter' became his most successful record.

George Melly (43): "My uncle loved Fats Waller and about 1934 I first heard his records on a maroon label. I was about 11 and I found songs like 'The Joint Is Jumpin'' immensely jolly and cheering. This was long before I had any concept of jazz."

Frank Robinson (44): "I've always preferred stride pianists. The cool pianists who play block chords all over the place don't excite me at all. James P. Johnson was the master: 'Carolina Shout' and all the others are wonderful stuff. I also love Fats Waller, Earl Hines, Joe Sullivan and Ralph Sutton. I like Jelly Roll Morton but he didn't swing like Waller, although he wrote lots of good tunes, which are favourites with many bands."

Fats Waller set the path for Louis Jordan who formed a jump band and sang fast-moving novelty songs with blue lyrics, the jazz equivalent of George Formby. Jordan with his self-mocking humour was very hip and fans might have hailed a passing Cab with a 'Hi-De-Ho'. Cab Calloway with his knowing 'Minnie The Moocher' and 'Reefer Man' and his zoot suits with loon pants was seen as both trendy and humorous.

John Chilton (45): "There is a family joke in our house in that I set out to see Louis Jordan, whose music I loved. I was telling my wife that I was going to see him and it was the last pea-souper fog that London had. I couldn't get there and I had to turn back. Not many other people got there either and it was a very poorly attended concert at Fairfield Hall, Croydon."

The Depression had affected music-making in the late 20s and early 30s as there was much less disposable income and musicians found it harder to get work. The song 'Brother, Can You Spare A Dime?' succinctly summarises the times.

The key to success was in being danceable and during the 1930s, there were hundreds of bands, both big and small, playing different strands of dance music. Liquor was prohibited in many states and this led to a profusion of illicit drinking clubs, the speakeasys. This, however, is a bit like the music in the brothels. Why did the bootleggers want to draw attention to their activities with loud music? In 1933 when prohibition was repealed, the attendance at the speakeasys declined. Dance music continued, however, and the key phrase from 1937 was Swing is King, and the swing bands, like Glenn Miller's, with their precise playing were gaining acceptance over more improvised music.

It was let's face the music and dance during the Second World War and there was still musical progress. Up until 1939, the guitar had not been a major feature of an orchestra because of its difficulty in being heard over the brass and the drums. Charlie Christian with his electric guitar changed all that. Bebop came along in the 1940s: its proponents dressed like smart businessmen and cool was the word. It became the favoured music of beat writers like Jack Kerouac.

Humphrey Lyttelton (46): "I get impatient with people who say, 'I don't listen to this stuff; I don't understand it.' Well, you never will understand it if you don't listen to it. You should listen to things as an exercise. Put on a Charlie Parker record for 15 minutes and along the way you will find something that is pretty acceptable."

XI

Lu Watters, who was born in 1910, had been working in music all his adult life, and by the late 1930s, he knew that he wanted to revive the two-trumpet sound of King Oliver and Louis Armstrong. He also knew how he wanted his band to sound and who he wanted in it. They included Bob Scobey and Turk Murphy with Clancy Hayes as the vocalist. Lu Watters wrote 'Big Bear Stomp' after the Big Bear Tavern in Redwood Canyon near Oakland, California, where their style developed during all night sessions.

Watters found a disused venue with a large dance floor, the Dawn Club in San Francisco, which had been a speakeasy. It was ideal for his band, the Yerba Buena Band, which played very lively music and which was named after an island in San Francisco Bay. They became very popular and the club became a regular haunt for Hollywood personalities. The cast of 'The Maltese Falcon' would gravitate to the Dawn Club and as well as Humphrey Bogart and John Huston, Orson Welles was also a regular. One of their best known pieces celebrated the club's address, 'Minstrels Of Annie Street'.

This led to a mini-revival of New Orleans music, although some of the first practitioners were not in a position to benefit. King Oliver, a forgotten man, had worked as a caretaker in a pool room before his death in 1938 at the age of 52. On the other hand, Bunk Johnson came out of retirement with a new set of teeth.

The Dawn Club had its own problems and closed in 1948. Watters moved his band to Sally Rand's club in El Cerrito. This had been a dance hall and a brothel - there were many small rooms to which patrons could go. He renamed the club, Hambone Kelly's, and was back in business. Lu Watters repertoire included 'Creole Belles', '1919 Rag', 'Emperor Norton's Hunch' and Armstrong favourites like 'Dippermouth Blues' and 'Cake Walking Babies (From Home)'. Clancy Hayes took the vocal on the humorous 'Huggin' And Chalkin'', which is about a girl who tips the scales at 22 stone, and 'I've Got A Bimbo'.

Turk Murphy could write in unusual keys. 'Duff Campbell's Revenge' was written for Eddie Condon and was in the difficult key of D flat. Turk wittily named it after a friend who hated Condon. At one stage Murphy wanted to put a stop to a trombonist who was copying everything he did. He decided to write a very difficult tune in a very difficult key, which he called 'Trombone Rag'. The plan would have succeeded if Turk could have played it himself.

John Lawrence (47): "Lu Watters decided to follow the lead of the King Oliver band but they also wrote a lot of original tunes. They were certainly a springboard for the Merseys, but we have never copied them slavishly. We have used them as a starting point."

Robin Tankard (48) : "There was a great resurgence of New Orleans music with the Lu Watters band and the Merseys were very influenced by them. The Merseys had never had a tuba player and I was determined to record 'Whitewash Man' and all the rags with them." (This is not completely accurate. Derek Vaux did play the tuba for a short while in the late 1960s, but stopped after giving himself a double hernia. However, the Merseys were not recording during this period.)

Phil Taylor (49): "My favourite band was the Yerba Buena Jazz Band in California. The Merseys have tried to be the same as them but now I think they're better."

Derek Vaux (50): "Most of my contemporaries at school liked New Orleans jazz and they liked the 'moldy fygge' sound, which is the oldest form of jazz and hence, considered to be its purest form. That square sound New Orleans jazz as played by Ken Colyer doesn't excite me at all. I did play with Ken Colyer for a short while but I left of my own free will very quickly because it was so boring and I hated it with a passion. I much preferred the music of Lu Watters and I've always liked the sound the Merseys made."

Umbrella Parade, 1999 style

Max Kaminsky (Dixieland trumpeter), makes a point to Ken Baldwin, John Lawrence and Jazz critic, Steve Voce

35

The Merseysippi Jazz Band

Left to right.—Seated (front): Dick Goodwin (bass); Don Lydiat (clarinet), Trevor Carlisle (drums), Frank Robinson (piano), Ken Baldwin (banjo), John Parkes (trombone), Pete Daniels (trumpet), Johnny Lawrence (trumpet). Centre: Louis Armstrong, with whom the Merseysippi played at Liverpool Stadium several years ago.

BORN on St. Valentine's Day 12 years ago, the Merseysippi Jazz Band, of Liverpool, is firmly established as one of Britain's most famous provincial semi-pro bands.

They have appeared on television and broadcast on radio; have played at London's Royal Festival Hall in a traditional jazz festival alongside Britain's top professional groups, and have cut five LPs.

A band with such drawing power and reputation would normally be expected to turn professional but the Merseysippi have determinedly remained semi-pro.

Says bass player and manager DICK GOODWIN:

"By avoiding the nerve strain of being together all the time, as the full-time professional band must, we have avoided the break-ups and constant changing of personnel which is such a feature of the business.

"We have had the advantage of staying together as our ideas and technique developed. By turning professional we feel we would lose a great deal of the enjoyment we get from playing now."

Dick is one of the three original members of the group still with the band.

The others are KEN BALD-

'The world's greatest two-trumpet band'

MM band spot

WIN on banjo, and pianist FRANK ROBINSON.

Clarinettist DON LYDIAT, rated one of the best men on his instrument in the country, joined the band in 1949, and trumpeter JOHNNY LAWRENCE came in the following year.

In the autumn of 1950, the Merseysippi indulged in the most intensive three-month rehearsal in its history. Like most jazz groups, it started with a model and, after becoming immersed in its idiom, tried to evolve a style of its own. The model was the Lu Watters band.

But it was in 1952, with the arrival of another trumpeter, PETE DANIELS, that the band began to get the sound

for which it became famous.

Noted for his playing and for his wit as band compère, Pete completed a two-trumpet front-line that subsequently caused many visitors to call it the greatest two-trumpet jazz band in the world.

Both trumpeters idolise Louis Armstrong — and the band always rates the highlight of its career the night it played with Satchmo at Liverpool Stadium.

TREVOR CARLISLE, on drums, and JOHN PARKES —a successor to Frank Parr, now with Mick Mulligan—were the only newcomers in the late 'fifties, though the band then began to feature singer CLINTON FORD as regular guest. He is back with them again this winter.

How long will the band last? Says Dick Goodwin: "We won't last for ever . . . but at the moment there is no sign of anyone wanting to retire."

CHAPTER 2
THE MUSIC GOES ROUND AND ROUND
Liverpool - UK jazz to 1950

I

King John knew what was happening north of Watford as he granted Liverpool its charter in 1207. It was being used as a harbour for sending supplies to Ireland, but because of strong tides, it did not develop as a port. Several centuries went by and then, through its unique geographical position, it came into its own with the industrial revolution and the growth of trade with American colonies. This enabled Liverpool's merchants to benefit from the import of raw materials and the export of finished goods but there was a less desirable enterprise in slave trading.

The ships sailed from Liverpool or Bristol and took cheap metal implements, trinkets and liquor to the west of Africa which were exchanged for slaves. The slaves were transported to the West Indies or to the southern states of America and the money from the sale purchased rum, sugar or cotton for the return journey to England. By the start of the 19th century, there was an anti-slavery movement which threatened the port with ruin, but even when slavery was abolished, the port continued to thrive. By and large, the trade look place in Liverpool and the ships were built over the water in Birkenhead, and the population grew from 200,000 in 1831 to 600,000 in 1891.

The first dock had been built in 1708 but the docklands developed during the 19th century. The Albert Dock, which was opened by the Prince Consort in 1845, was the first English dock to have warehouse facilities on site. If I go to the Heritage Market at Stanley Dock, I look up and see the sheer enormity of the warehouses: it gives me a feeling of how prosperous Liverpool was and how confident the merchants were when it was built at the entrance to the Leeds-Liverpool canal in 1848.

Liverpool is also a city of commerce. Royal Insurance was formed in 1845 simply because a group of Liverpool businessmen thought that they were being overcharged by London companies. The best known landmark on the Liverpool skyline is the Royal Liver

Building, which was built in 1910 and belongs to another successful insurance company. At the top of each of its two towers is a Liver Bird, which is a close cousin of a comorant. It is said that the city will fall when the two birds fly away. No chance of that.

II

In 1984 I wrote a book, 'Let's Go Down The Cavern' and the publishers insisted that a comment by Ken Dodd, likening the city to a packet of Smarties, be removed from the final text. I never understood why this was considered racist and indeed Ken Dodd was making a witty and pertinent statement about the city. There is a wide ethnic and cultural mix here. English, Irish and Welsh predominate, but there is also a Chinatown and thousands of citizens with Caribbean or African ancestry. John Lennon told 'Rolling Stone' in 1970: "We were the ones that were looked down upon as animals by the southerners, the Londoners. The northerners in the States think people are pigs down south. Liverpool was a very poor city but tough. People have a sense of humour because they are in such pain. They are very witty, and it's an Irish place. It's where the Irish came when they ran out of potatoes, and it's where the blacks worked as slaves or whatever." I don't think we had slaves in Liverpool but you know what he means. Lennon added, "America is where it's at. I regret profoundly that I was not an American and not born in Greenwich Village." This quotation has been conveniently overlooked in all the John Lennon celebrations in Liverpool.

Liverpool is a city of culture, highlighted by the Liverpool Museum, the Walker Art Galley and the Picton Library, which are all in William Brown Street and were all built in the mid-19th century. Opposite them is the splendid St George's Hall, which was built, apparently back to front, in 1839. In 1870 these buildings were joined by Lime Street Station, which gave another boost to the city's prosperity.

The port did not have a cathedral until the 20th century when it acquired two. The work on the Anglican cathedral began in 1904 and although the enormous building was soon operating as a place of worship, the work was not completed until 1978. The Roman Catholic cathedral, known locally as Paddy's Wigwam and the

Mersey Funnel, was built in the 1960s, being completed in 1967.

The Royal Liverpool Philharmonic Society began in 1840 and the city has a reputation for attracting high quality productions and performers. My favourite moment occurred in 1874 when the organisers of the Liverpool Festival invited Franz Liszt to play. He wrote back, "You are presumably unaware that for 26 years I have altogether ceased to be regarded as a pianist." Oops.

Liverpool is famous for its humour and there has been a stream of famous comedians from the area including Arthur Askey, Robb Wilton, Tommy Handley, Ted Ray and Ken Dodd. A contributing factor in the Beatles' success must have been their instinctive Liverpool wit and indeed, the best known joke at a Royal Variety Peformance - the one about rattling your jewellery - did not come from a professional comic but from John Lennon.

The city is also considered sentimental, perhaps illustrated by Lonnie Donegan's remark that he could sing a song about a blind orphan, 'Nobody's Child', to great effect in Liverpool whereas no one would take much notice of it in London.

From time to time, comparisons are made linking Liverpool to New Orleans. Certainly both cities are ports and both cities have shameful pasts through the slave trade, but, as a result, both cities are now cosmopolitan. Jazz began in New Orleans in 1895 and Mersey Beat in Liverpool in 1962. The world's most successful jazz musician, Louis Armstrong, came from New Orleans and the world's most successful songwriters, Lennon and McCartney, came from Liverpool. There is one major difference: one city was embracing jazz and the other rejecting it.

In the 1980s, the Mayor of New Orleans wrote to the Lord Mayor of Liverpool suggesting a twinning of the cities. After the dignitaries had met each other, there would be some musical exchanges. It was an apt suggestion but nothing came of it. However, in 2001, both New Orleans and Liverpool renamed their airports after one of their musical sons - namely, Louis Armstrong and John Lennon. It is not yet possible to fly direct from Armstrong to Lennon or vice versa, but the time will come.

III

Jazz originated in America and by most accounts, it arrived in Britain when that ship carrying the Original Dixieland Jazz Band docked in Liverpool in 1919. Much as I love this story, I am sure that jazz was around before then. A successful act would not have come to Britain on a whim: the promoter must have recognised an audience for this music. Hence, there must have been some interest in jazz before they came, and perhaps the music had reached us via sailors and music publishers.

Intriguingly, the Original Dixieland Jazz Band disembarked in Liverpool on April Fool's Day, 1919. If they had performed in the city, it would have represented the first professional performance by an American jazz band in the UK. Instead, they moved to London and a variety show with George Robey topping the bill. He was no Prime Minister of Mirth when he found that these upstarts were generating more applause than himself. He insisted that they be removed from the show. As the revue depended on Robey, the jazzers went elsewhere and continued their success at the London Palladium. They did much to introduce jazz to Europe, but they lost ground in America once King Oliver and Louis Armstrong were recording.

Whatever, the Original Dixieland Jazz Band made a great impression as they stayed for 15 months - what happened to their bookings in America? - and performed before royalty as George V was intrigued to learn more about tiger rags and ostrich walks. Many reviews were approving, but others sound like the critics who denounced rock'n'roll in the 50s: "I can see clearly that if I can rattle on any old tin, my future will be made."

Critics were kinder in their approval of the Southern Syncopated Orchestra, which arrived shortly after the ODJB, on 14 June 1919. As there were race riots in Liverpool, they swiftly moved on. A review in the 'Daily Herald' praised their performance for being "real ragtime played by real darkies". The magazine, 'Revue Romance', noted their "astonishing perfection, superb taste and fervour" and the critic added, "I wish to set down the name of this artist of genius, as for myself I shall never forget it: Sidney Bechet." In 1922, Bechet was charged with attempted rape, found guilty and deported. A female writer in the 'Sunday Chronicle' might have had this in mind when she condemned jazz music, concluding, "Before mothers give permission to their girls to go alone to jazz dances let them know first where they are going, or else go with them."

A creole, Bechet, who played clarinet and soprano sax, also made the journey from New Orleans to Chicago and he worked in his early years with both Louis Armstrong and Duke Ellington. In the late 1920s he settled in Paris. He often recorded jazz standards, but he also wrote two hits from the trad era - 'Petite Fleur' and 'Lonesome (Si Tu Vois Ma Mère)'.

The periodical, 'Melody Maker', began in 1926, initially an organ for songs published by Lawrence Wright. It quickly became an important publication for promoting performances and records by jazz performers, although it preferred white dance bands. Such was the interest in jazz that a specialist record shop, Levy's, opened in London in 1927.

There were many dance bands in the UK playing the popular songs of the day. From time to time, they might play jazz tunes and a notable example of this crossover is the Rhythmic Eight who recorded 260 titles between 1927 and 1932, many of them jazz tunes. Their personnel, interestingly, included both British and American musicians. In 1927 a Cambridge University jazz band, the Quinquaginta Ramblers, received some publicity, and their tenor saxophonist, Maurice Allom, found cricketing fame three years later by achieving a hat-trick on his first appearance in a Test Match.

Louis Armstrong first came to the UK in 1932. He arrived on his own and was teamed with some French musicians (itself a telling comment on the state of UK jazz) for his debut at the London Palladium. Armstrong was extremely well received, although Hannen Swaffer in the 'Daily Herald' insulted him: "Armstrong is the ugliest man I have ever seen on the music hall stage. He looks and behaves like an untrained gorilla." And much more. When some readers complained, he wrote, "Armstrong is by no means angry with my reference to his looks. After all he has seen himself in the glass several times and got used to it."

Duke Ellington came over with his orchestra the following year and appeared at the Palladium with the 'cheeky chappie' comedian, Max Miller. Ellington was universally acclaimed, although some critics found his music too loud. Coleman Hawkins, Cab Calloway and Joe Venuti also crossed the Atlantic and there were performances by the French gypsy guitarist, Django Reinhardt. American performers enjoyed coming to the UK, but the Musicians' Union heeded some of its members who felt that they were being deprived of work by American performers. Nonsense of course as these musicians promoted jazz music in the UK and the supporting bills for their concerts featured home-grown talent. In their arrogance, it never occurred to the Musicians' Union that the general public might want to hear the American performers. The union persuaded the Ministry of Labour that American musicians should not be allowed into the UK until a reciprocal agreement had been reached with the American Federation of Musicians. A tit for tat arrangement was impracticable as no British musicians had the talent and pulling power of Armstrong or Ellington. Effectively, American musicians could only work on stage as variety performers or as part of a theatrical production.

During the war, some American servicemen who were also musicians sat in with various British bands and also made recordings. After some discussion with the Musicians' Union and the Ministry of Labour, Duke Ellington and Benny Goodman appeared in the UK at the end of the 1940s, although they had to work with British musicians. Their work permits said that they were 'variety artists' rather than 'jazzmen'. **Ken Pitt (51)**: "The bands couldn't work here at all. The first American band to come here as part of an exchange deal was Stan Kenton's with Vic Lewis' orchestra in exchange. I can remember the Nat 'King' Cole trio coming over here and the work permit said that they were jugglers. I don't think they did any juggling at all."

IV

The first British jazz star was the trumpeter Nat Gonella. He played with dance bands like Billy Cotton and Roy Fox and left Lew Stone in 1935 to work with a small jazz band, the Georgians. Quite unusually, he made records in the US and many regarded him as a British Armstrong. As Steve Race wrote in 'Jazz News' in 1961,

"There is no such thing as British jazz. There is only American jazz played by British musicians."

There was considerable opposition to jazz on the BBC and the first regular jazz programme wasn't until 'Radio Rhythm Club', which began in 1940, and became 'BBC Jazz Club' in 1947. Its resident band, the Radio Rhythm Club Sextet, made many records and included many notable musicians including George Shearing. Shearing, a pianist and composer, was the first British musician who could compete at the highest level. He often worked in the UK with Stephane Grappelli but he found a greater appreciation for his work in America and emigrated in 1947.

Kenny Ball (52): "In 1943, I joined the sea cadets and got a bugle, but you can only play five notes on a bugle. I thought of the trumpet instead because Betty Grable was going with Harry James. I picked up the trumpet to get the crumpet. Didn't work that well, but Harry James was a great jazz player and is very underrated by the purists. He made some wonderful boogie woogie recordings. One had 'Boo Woo' on one side and 'Woo Woo' on the other."

Chris Barber (53): "I played violin when I was a kid but I had to give it up because I've got a slight curvature of the spine and playing the violin hurt me in the small of my back. My parents didn't believe me and they thought it was an excuse not to practice. When I was called up, I was turned down as Grade 4 so at least I was vindicated, and also I didn't have to go into the forces which was very nice."

John Parkes (54): "I didn't take up the trombone till I was 21. Before that I was a piano player and I was called up for the mines when I was 18. I wanted to go in the RAF but Ernest Bevin, the Minister of Labour, put the numbers 0 to 9 in a hat and asked an office boy to pick a number. He picked '0' and anybody whose national registration ended in zero went down the mines, and there was no way out, you had to go. It was known as 'Calling Johnny Zeroes'. Maybe I wouldn't be talking to you if it had gone the other way. It was awful because I'm tall and the seam was very low indeed and wet and on a slant. I had four years of crawling about in that. I was the only piano player in a hostel of 700 fellers, all Bevin boys, and I did do some piano playing for evening dances. I got on some shifts that allowed me to do that, so I was luckier than some."

In 1943 a group of amateur musicians, George Webb's Dixielanders, began playing on Monday evenings at the Red Barn at Barnehurst, Kent. George Webb played piano and Wally Fawkes on clarinet modelled his style on Sidney Bechet's. With Reg Rigden and Owen Bryce, they developed a two-trumpet sound. The trombone player, Eddie Harvey, was accused of having a dance band style but instead of being dismissed, he was asked to justify himself at a kangaroo court. There's no doubt that George Webb's Dixielanders were an exciting live band and this led to revivalist bands throughout the country.

Jim Godbolt (55): "The Revivalist movement, which was based on the concept that the best jazz comes from New Orleans, started with George Webb's Dixielanders in the mid-1940s. They didn't have any thoughts of becoming well-known or influential, but they became both. They spearheaded the traditionalist jazz movement in this country - it was in a very rough and ready way, but at the time we all thought it was marvellous. There were other bands like Freddy Randall's in Walthamstow and Ken Smiley's in Belfast, but none of those bands had the same impact as George Webb's Dixielanders. They were playing well outside of London but they became a cult attraction with people turning up from all parts of London and indeed the country to hear them play in the basement bar of the Red Barn."

The Dixielanders found a wider following through London concerts promoted by the Young Communist League. Then they promoted their own concerts under the banner of the Hot Club of London in Tottenham Court Road. On one evening in January 1947, Humphrey Lyttelton made his concert debut. Lyttelton then replaced Reg Rigden in the Dixielanders, but Owen Bryce couldn't match the talent of his new partner. Lyttelton left in November 1947, thereby ending George Webb's Dixielanders, and starting up his own band with Wally Fawkes on clarinet and saxophone. Lyttelton secured a recording contract with Parlophone and became popular nationally.

Humphrey Lyttelton (56): "A lot of my ancestors were very, very important people: there are cabinet ministers, archbishops, headmasters and generals in there but the only one that I readily identify with is the first Humphrey Lyttelton who was hanged after the Gunpowder Plot. I thought, 'Here's someone who was a bit out of the ordinary, and sometimes when I started playing the trumpet, I was regarded by the stuffier members of the family - not my parents, who were good about it, but by the others - in rather the same light as the one who was trying to blow up the Houses of Parliament. One of Wally's ancestors was Guy Fawkes, so that might have drawn us to each other, I don't know. We met up when I joined George Webb's Dixielanders and he found me a job as an illustrator at the 'Daily Mail'. It wasn't simply Humphrey Lyttelton's band, but Humph and Wally's. Wally left around 1956 because we had to decide whether to become fully professional. We were doing too much touring for him to hold down a full-time job doing the strip cartoon, 'Flook'."

Chris Barber (57): "I used to go and see Humph's band every week and I would always sit at the front. One day the trombone player asked me if I wanted to buy his trombone 'cause he had a better one coming. It was six and a half quid, which I thought was fair enough, but it wasn't even worth two quid. It was a terrible instrument tied together with string. All the joints came undone when I started to play it."

John Parkes (58): "When I took up the trombone, my teacher would tell me, 'Don't puff your cheeks out'. You have a set of muscles around your mouth and you should have everything guided towards that. Then I would see pictures of George Chisholm and he puffed his cheeks out the whole time. He was the greatest in the land, so I wasn't sure who was right."

Many jazz musicians began their professional careers in dance bands. **Ronnie Scott (59)**: "In 1946 I was lucky enough to get a job with Ted Heath and his Orchestra. The band played in Liverpool one night and had a gig in London the following day. Everybody but me caught the night train back after the gig, but I was earning what was a lot of money in those days and I decided to stay in a hotel and fly back the next day. Unfortunately, there was then the worst snowstorm that the country had seen in 30 years. The planes were grounded and the only way to get back was by train, which made me too late for the gig. Shortly afterwards, I got a letter from Ted Heath telling me that my services were no longer required."

George Melly (60): "My worst gig was with Mick Mulligan in the South Harrow Youth Club. We played very badly, but we were only starting. Our audience consisted of six lads of between 7 and 10, and after our first number they looked as us incredulously as we were making this terrible noise. It was still at the time of rationing in the late 40s. One lad put his head round the door and said, 'Chocolate biscuits in the canteen', and they all scarpered off."

Some musicians wanted to play the more experimental bebop that was coming into vogue in the US. The tenor saxophonist Ronnie Scott played this music at Club Eleven, which led to Ronnie Scott's Club. The accordionist, Tito Burns, made the record, 'Bebop Spoken Here', but gave up playing to become an agent, discovering Cliff Richard in 1958. Louis Armstrong was uneasy about bebop, parodying it in his version of 'The Whiffenpoof Song' in 1954. Two camps formed: one for traditonal and one for what became known as modern jazz.

Ronnie Scott (61): "I don't like the term 'modern jazz'. I prefer 'contemporary jazz' and hopefully, we were playing the kind of jazz that was contemporary. We were listening to Dizzy Gillespie and Charlie Parker. It was a very good band with Victor Feldman, Derek Humble and Phil Seamen and the records that we made stand up very well."

In1948 the National Federation of Jazz Organisations of Great Britain and Northern Ireland (NFJO) was established to further jazz interests in the UK. They argued that it was in the interests of British musicians to allow Americans to perform here, but such arguments convinced neither the Musicians' Union nor the Ministry of Labour. In 1949 the promoter Bert Wilcox and his associates invited Sidney Bechet to play in concert in an unbilled (but widely promoted) appearance with Humphrey Lyttelton and his band. Bechet's role in the duplicity is uncertain as he was given a fake work permit from someone who had worked in the Foreign Office. On arrival, he had broken his dentures and had trouble with a stomach ulcer. Possibly, they were excuses not to perform, but

Wilcox found a dentist and a doctor and ensured that Bechet made the concert. He sat in the audience, Humph introduced him, and the audience begged him to play. Appropriately enough, the first number was 'Weary Blues'. Bechet also recorded illegally with Lyttelton's band while he was here. Bert Wilcox was prosecuted for breaking the law. The defence and, indeed, the prosecution highlighted the absurdity of the situation but Wilcox and his associates had contravened the Aliens Act (which sounds as if the Government was expecting an outer space invasion) and were fined £300

CHARIVARIA

WE understand that a proposal to send a relief party to America to rescue Scotsmen from the threatened Prohibition law is under consideration.

⁎

It is rumoured that *The Times* is about to announce that it does not hold itself responsible for editorial opinions expressed in its own columns.

⁎

A correspondent, complaining of the tiny flats in London, states that he is a trombone-player, and every time he wants to get the lowest note he has to go out on to the landing.

⁎

In Essex Street, Shoreditch —so Dr. ADDISON explained to the House of Commons—there are seven hundred and thirty-three people in twenty-nine houses. A correspondent writes that a single house in the neighbourhood of Big Ben contains seven hundred and seven persons, many of them incapable, and that nothing is being done about it.

⁎

"The Original Dixie Land Jazz Band has arrived in London," says an evening paper. We are grateful for the warning. *⁎*

"Punch", 1919

47

CHAPTER 3
AND IT COMES OUT HERE
Formation of Merseysippi Jazz Band

The first members of the Merseysippi Jazz Band were born around 1930 but only **Don Lydiatt (62)**, and his schoolfriend, Ken Baldwin, grew up listening to jazz music: "My brother collected Artie Shaw and Benny Goodman records and when someone older than you says that this is the best, you tend to believe him. In 1938, when I was 11 or 12, my mother bought me a little E flat clarinet. The first thing I learnt was Barney Bigard's 'Lull At Dawn' which was a very simple little thing and then Artie Shaw's 'Frenesi'. During the bebop era, I became impressed with Charlie Parker and Dizzy Gillespie and their extended chords and I bought myself a tenor saxophone and tried to play like that. I was called up and after the war, I was part of the King Quintet and we went in for the 'Melody Maker' dance band championship. We won a heat in Manchester and went on to the North Britain semi-final. We were judged by proper musicians and we were pleased to come third, but it was only the first two bands who went to the finals at the Royal Albert Hall. Freddy Randall's band came out of that competition. The King Quintet didn't last long because the pianist was a medical student and the guitarist went to London. I was married by then and it never even dawned on me to go professional as I was much too cautious."

Because of the Musicians' Union restrictions, most teenagers hadn't been able to see any American musicians live and there had been precious little jazz on the radio.

Frank Parr (63): "I went to Wallasey Grammar School and during the war, you only had one jazz 78rpm issued per month. I got hold of one and liked the sound of it and my interest in jazz started there. The record in question was Bob Crosby's 'Five Point Blues' featuring the trumpet player Yank Lawson. It sounded so different from the usual load of crap that you heard on the radio."

John Lawrence (64): "I was in the army and I met someone who was very interested in jazz and I still remember the first jazz record he played me which was one of the Muggsy Spanier recordings, 'At The Jazz Band Ball'. I thought it sounded a tremendously confused mess, but he persisted and after a few evenings of listening to them, I realised that there was more in this than I realised and I got interested."

Ralph Watmough (65): "We had a band at Merchant Taylors' School called the Crosby Rhythm Kings. This was composed almost entirely of members of the school except for the tuba player who came from Southport and used to play with us on all our outside gigs. We were playing at the Crosby Carnival on a float in a procession and we were playing away merrily and we turned a corner and there was our form master staring at us in horror. We thought that we would be reported to the headmaster and expelled but fortunately he took the right attitude and nothing was said. The band floundered when we left school. We did reform briefly after National Service and then the band broke up and I picked up the pieces and formed my own band."

Ralph Watmough (66) also recalls the Merseys' current bass player at Merchant Taylors': "A little bit behind us was Derek Vaux. He was three years younger than me. We had a room at the back of the school house that was separate from the rest of the school. This was when we were in the sixth form and it was very convenient for jam sessions at lunchtime. Very few people came up there but I can remember Derek, who must have been 13, poking his head round the door to see what was going on and being chased off with 'Go away, you horrible little boy.'"

There was the occasional concert by British jazz musicians on Merseyside, but it was very much a cottage industry. **Harold Culling (67)**: "When I was about 18 in 1947 or '48 and an apprentice electrician, I arranged a concert at the Picton Hall with Humphrey Lyttelton. It was a sell-out and then I got a phone call shortly before the concert telling me that somebody else had a contract with Lyttelton and he couldn't play within 12 miles of where he was playing for this other chap."

Dennis Gracey (68): "Harold Culling found himself with the hall booked and an artist who wasn't allowed to play, so what could he do? We stood outside the Picton Hall and as the people arrived, we returned their money and took their tickets from them. Then we all went to the Stork Hotel in Clayton Square and Humph played on the top floor with all the windows open and the crowd who would have been at the concert were listening in the square below. That was a wonderful evening and although the Council refunded most of Harold's money, he did lose out on it."

Harold Culling (69): "Humph said he could play at the Stork Club where we had the Rhythm Club meetings and we had a full room. We got £40 in the collection which did little to cover my expenses. It put me off organising other concerts and I feel I could have been doing great things today if I hadn't lost my money on that."

Jazz fans of the day were buying records and sharing them with their friends at regular meetings, often called Rhythm Clubs. You needed to have someone with a good collection behind any club.

John Lawrence (70): "When I came out of the army, my father who had a cork business - bottle corks and all cork products - asked me to join the business. It sounded like a cushy number and so I said yes, and he said, 'Right, you can go to Liverpool.' It's a sad thing to have been conned by your own father but the business had a branch in Liverpool and there was a gap in the Liverpool staff which he wanted me to fill. I came up here and I bless the moment I did because I have had all this fun with the band and it's enriched my whole life. My musical life, my social life, my marriage all sprang from being in the band. It all started when I met the members of the Wallasey Rhythm Club, which was a record collectors club. We used to meet every week and I became hooked. There were no musicians in it then, but listening to any sort of jazz was quite an achievement really."

Ken Baldwin (71): "Jazz records were difficult to come by: it was just after the war, few of them were released here and the shops didn't import them. If you happened to have a relation in the navy, he might bring back a record or two, and this could be played and discussed at a meeting."

Merseyside collector **Harold Culling (72)** again: "I think the Americans brought over popular music and not jazz. Americans seemed to ignore their own natural music, the jazz music. They used to bring a lot of rubbish over, dance bands and the like. I found importing records very satisfying as I could get records that I couldn't get here, sometimes I could sell them and sometimes I could keep them. I have still got some of them now. The collection still expands and luckily I have a wife who thinks the same as me."

Dennis Gracey (73): "Harold Culling did more to bring jazz to Liverpool than anybody else. He used to import records from America and he would get a delivery every month. They would be shellac records packed in sawdust. We had never heard music like this. Then he began to get American V-discs which were like LPs but made exclusively for the American forces over here, and I remember hearing Eddie Condon's New York concerts with all the stars of the day. We had only heard music that was perfectly orchestrated before and this was wonderful live music. I love live music today and studio contrived music doesn't always come off."

The Wallasey Rhythm Club prospered. **John Lawrence (74)**: "We started meeting in each other's houses and Dick Goodwin decided that we should move to bigger premises so that more people could attend. We then met every week at the Hotel Victoria in New Brighton and we were getting 20, 30 or 40 people turning up. As a result of listening to records, one or two people got interested in playing, and at the end of each week's meeting, someone would play the piano or the guitar, and it built up from there."

Bob Gough (75): "It sounds real anorak stuff, but there was no other way to listen to the records then or find out something about the performers. I would get the underground train from Liverpool to New Brighton and it would be thrilling to hear the latest American release by Kid Ory or to listen to someone talking about Duke Ellington or Bunk Johnson. At first, the live music was just Ken Baldwin and Frank Robinson playing something at the end of the session."

Dennis Gracey (76): "We were all interested in jazz. Don Lydiatt played the clarinet and Bruce Fletcher played trumpet in the early days, with Dr Miller on piano and Ken Baldwin with his banjo. I played the trombone very very badly, but we thought we were great, we thought we were marvellous because we believed in the music. I only played a trombone because nobody else was playing the trombone. It cost me five shillings from a shop in London Road. It was very very cheap and it was full of holes which I used to fill up by using very thick cream on the slide. These were primitive days.

Through Harold Culling the band heard of Lu Watters and that formed the basis of the repertoire. We played 'Smokey Mokes' and 'At The Jazz Band Ball'."

By Christmas 1948, Dick Goodwin wanted to form a full jazz band. **Ken Baldwin (77)**: "The guy who got the band together was Dick Goodwin who played bass and was a member of the club. He contacted people whom he thought might be interested in playing. He knew that I played a bit of guitar and banjo and so he rang me up. I used to go to school with a boy who used to bring his clarinet and sax to school when he was 14 or 15, and he was a natural. We knew a piano player, Frank Robinson, but we needed a trumpet player. Dick saw a group of street musicians and he approached the trumpet player, Wally Fisher. The only jazz number he knew was 'At The Jazz Band Ball'. Dick heard this and automatically thought he was an expert in jazz, which proved to be far from the case."

Ralph Watmough (78): "I formed the Crosby Rhythm Kings in 1948 just before the Merseysippi Jazz Band was formed. There was a network of rhythm clubs where people met in cellars and back rooms and played records and discussed them and the one in Crosby was the Crosby Rhythm Club. One of the officials and myself went over to the Wallasey Rhythm Club at the Hotel Victoria. We did the usual thing of seriously listening to all this music and um'ing and ah'ing with profound knowledge and in the interval a band appeared and it turned out to be the Merseys in the course of its birth pangs. We hadn't got used to hearing amateur bands and we regarded them as a bit of a joke, but then people did the same with us."

Frank Robinson (79) is one of the Merseys' founder members: "I was told that when I was about three years of age, my family would put on the gramophone and I would pretend to be playing on the top of the chair, so everyone thought I was going to be a piano player, and that's what happened. My sister, who was older than me, was a piano tutor and she had pupils coming to the house and going through the scales, and I was always cocking an ear to this."

Ken Baldwin (80): "My mum and dad played piano but my eldest brother was 17 years older than me, and he had a houseful of instruments - flutes, clarinets, violins, banjos, guitar, mandolin. He would practice them avidly for about six months and when he found that they weren't as easy to play as he thought, he'd move on to something else and try that for a bit. I used to be an enormous fan of George Formby's and when I was 11 and passed my scholarship, my parents bought me a ukulele-banjo. I played it for years and then as my hands got bigger, I tried my brother's guitar which was a bit difficult. He also had an old zither banjo that had come out of the Ark and I found that easier. I was borrowing his instruments until I could afford one of my own, and I was playing that old zither banjo in the band in 1949."

Ken addressed everybody, male or female, as 'Nob' and this caught on with everybody calling everybody else in the band 'Nob' from time to time. There is only one 'Nob' though, Ken Baldwin himself. I'm wary about doing a serious history of the band with a man called Nob so I am referring to him throughout as **Ken Baldwin (81)**: "When I was in the army, I picked up this habit of calling people Nob, and it had something to do with the fact that I can't remember names too well. It is extremely convenient and it has served me well throughout my life. If I can't remember who it is, I say, 'Oh, Nob, it is nice to see you again.'"

The newly formed jazz group played its first date as the Wallasey Rhythm Kings at a Valentine's Day dance in 1949. It was promoted as 'Merseyside's First Jazz Band Ball'. Admission was three shillings (15p), refreshments could be purchased 'at moderate prices' and dancing was from 7.30 pm to 11.30 pm. The Wallasey Rhythm Kings line-up was Wally Fisher (trumpet), Dennis Gracey (trombone), Evan Patrick (clarinet), Frank Robinson (piano), Ken Baldwin (banjo, guitar), Dick Goodwin (bass) and Ken Metcalfe (drums). **Frank Robinson (82)**: "The gig itself was in the Grosvenor Ballroom in Wallasey, and it was a jazz band ball. We were supporting the Smoky City Stompers from Manchester and we were very nervous about it. The first tune we played was naturally 'At The Jazz Band Ball'. A fellow called Bernard Garland had financed it, but the event made a profit and we took off from there." Indeed. The profit from the night was £2.1.9d (£2.09).

Ken Baldwin (83): "We learnt the standard jazz tunes - 'Basin Street Blues', 'At The Jazz Band Ball' -but we only knew six numbers. Our entire repertoire lasted only 20 minutes, although of course we could repeat tunes."

Dennis Gracey (84): "I remember the evening very well. We were supporting Eric Lister's Smoky City Stompers and we were only going to play a few numbers. However, they were late arriving so we ended up playing for a lot longer than we were supposed to."

John Lawrence (85): "The Smoky City Stompers came from Manchester and their clarinet player Eric Lister could only play in the key of F. They weren't much more advanced than us but I must say that Eric played very well in that one key. They also had a small group within the group who were called the Tassle Alley Washboard Creepers, Tassle Alley being a back crack around the area that they used to play."

The name, the Wallasey Rhythm Kings, didn't last long and a new name, the Merseysippi Jazz Band, came into being in April 1949. **Frank Robinson (86)**: "The original name didn't have any impact, so it was thrown open to the lads, 'Let's have another name', and when it came to my turn, I said, 'The music's from Mississippi and we're on the Mersey, so how about the Merseysippi Jazz Band?' Some members thought it was corny, but it stuck."

Ken Baldwin (87): "We didn't plan to stay with it as it was a silly name, but you do one gig and then another and then it gets too late to change it. We've all got used to it now and we like it. It is often misspelt in programmes - we get often Mersseysippi (sic)." (Frank Robinson also composed 'Merseysippi Rag' but he rarely plays it now: "I wrote it because 'Maple Leaf Rag' was too complicated for me at the time.")

Frank Robinson (88): "Our second paid gig was on the back of a truck in Ormskirk for its Rose Queen carnival. We were invited to play at a jazz band contest and we won it because no other band turned up and we got £5 for it."

Bob Gough (89): "You'll see me with the band on that truck and that's because Dick Goodwin asked me to come along to steady the bass as he felt it would wobble about as it moved. In the end, I was not sure if I was there to steady Dick or the bass."

Dennis Gracey (90): "We were all such bad musicians, but we were so involved with the music and we thought that we were ambassadors, trying to make people listen to this music. If you didn't like it, there was something wrong with you and we used to play very simple music, so we played the blues over and over again at different tempos because that's all we could play. The band couldn't play anything with a real melody to it for years, so we didn't have a big repertoire. We did a concert at St George's Hall with Freddy Randall's band and it was our first exposure to the public in a concert hall and we had learnt eight tunes. Unfortunately, Freddy Randall went on first and played most of them. We found ourselves floundering and having to play the same things, only not as well."

Live modern jazz was also getting a foothold through **Ross McManus (91)**, who sang and played trumpet. "I had come back from Egypt and we formed a group in Birkenhead, Ross McManus and his New Era Music. We were trying to do the bebop things and I could do a fairly good take off of Miles Davis, but a lot of the bookings depended on my singing really. It was a small group with Bert Green on piano, Tony Edwards on bass, Frank Platt on drums and George Carroll on tenor. George would huff and puff like a steam engine. This hissing noise used to come out of him as if driven by steam, but he was a tremendously powerful saxophone player. We did very well. We did the Grafton, the New Brighton Tower and the Kingsland, all big venues."

In September 1949, 'Wallasey Chronicle' told of "Another successful evening with the Merseysippi Jazz Band, on this occasion being joined by a visitor from London, George Melly, who surprised everybody with his powerful singing of some traditional blues including 'Frankie And Johnny'." **George Melly (92)**: "'Frankie And Johnny' was a folk ballad and it is in 'The Oxford Book Of Light Verse', edited by W.H. Auden. I first heard it by Frank Crumit and there are other versions such as 'Frankie And Albert' by Ma Rainey. I love it because it allows me to dramatise a lot. There is a bit where I used to imitate Johnny and Nellie Bligh making love. I would turn my back on the audience and embrace myself, an old vaudeville trick. I'm not the right shape to do that now, so I take off my shoes and put one over each shoulder, which makes it a rather more fashionable but esoteric form of love."

Bob Gough (93): "I remember George Melly turning up at the Hotel Vic with a letter from Derek Stuart-Baxter of the Melody Maker recommending George to Les Phythian of the Wallasey Rhythm Club and saying he was 'an interesting character'. I remember him singing 'Georgia Grind' and coming back with us on the train to Liverpool. As the train pulled out of the station, we started playing and we continued until we arrived in Liverpool. This became something of a ritual after the meetings."

Remember when you read this next quote that these are the years before rock'n'roll. **Dennis Gracey (94)**: "My mother and father thought I was a real rebel going out and playing jazz. This was not the thing to do and they frowned upon it. Evan Patrick came from a deeply religious family and we used to have to smuggle him out of the house on a Sunday."

Evan Patrick, who called himself Pat Evans when he was with the MJB, was the first to leave. **Ken Baldwin (95)**: "Evan Patrick was a good Welshman. He was about to study to be a doctor at Liverpool University, a four year course, and his parents didn't think that jazz and his studies mingled at all. He didn't last long with us, starting in February and going by end of the year." Evan Patrick qualified as a doctor and he is now retired and living in Canada.

Don Lydiatt (96): "The band formed in February 1949 and I joined in October. I got a letter from Frank Robinson asking me to join and I wasn't playing much clarinet at the time, it was mostly tenor sax. Tenor playing was a dirty word with many jazz fans. When Bruce Turner joined Humphrey Lyttelton, the dyed-in-the-wool fans came with placards saying, 'Go home dirty bopper', and yet all the jazz bands in the early 20s had saxophones. They had this limited, narrow view of what the music should be, and the saxophone was definitely out."

Humphrey Lyttelton ventured north on 5 February 1950, playing with the Merseys at the Tivoli Theatre in New Brighton. This inaugural concert for the Liverpool Jazz Club led to numerous guest visits from bands of the day. **Chris Barber (97)**: "We came by train the first time we came to play in Liverpool, which would be in 1950. We played a concert at the Picton Hall, and the banjo player and myself were walking along Lord Nelson Street and this person said,

'What have you got in that case, wack?' The instrument was not known to a lot of people."

John Higham (98): "The first jazz I heard was at school because I used to play snooker and the snooker table was by the gramophone. This lad who was a couple of years older than me kept playing records, mostly swing, but he put on Humphrey Lyttelton one night. I thought, 'That is a different sound, I like that', so I went to a Humphrey Lyttelton concert at the Picton Hall in Liverpool in 1950. I was bowled over and I have been trying to play the stuff he was playing ever since. Looking back, his technique was a bit rough in those days. It certainly didn't swing and he had a very plodding 1950s rhythm section, but as far as sincerity and passion were concerned, his playing exceeded everybody's expectations."

Big events were sometimes planned such as a Merseyside Festival of Jazz in 1950. This had been intended for the Philharmonic Hall but according to Rev H.D. Longbottom who was part of the city's Finance and General Purposes Committee, "We didn't think that jazz was suitable music for a hall of the Philharmonic's character - especially on a Sunday." This reaction was typical of the times - 'Daily Graphic' in February 1952 reported a licence which had been turned down for a concert by Mick Mulligan's Magnolia Jazz Band and the Merseys because the proposed set list included 'Send Me To The 'Lectric Chair', 'Gimme A Pigfoot' and, amazingly, 'When The Saints Go Marching In'. The theatre manager said afterwards, "The titles may sound a bit ghastly but it is an amusement for young people."

Having been refused the Philharmonic Hall, the festival took place at Liverpool Stadium on 2 April 1950. The Merseysippi Jazz Band played alongside an impressive lineup of the pianist Ralph Sharon, Kathy Stobart's New Music, Freddy Randall's Band, Mick Mulligan and his Magnolia Jazz Band, the Terry Walsh Bop Group and Terry Smith's Swing Group. The band did well but it was the final appearance for both Wally Fisher and Dennis Gracey.

Wally Fisher had a different temperament from the rest of the band. **Ken Baldwin (99)**: "Wally Fisher had been a merchant seaman but he was unemployed at the time. I worked for the Mersey Docks

And Harbour Board and I told him that as he'd been a regular seaman, he could hold down a regular job as an AB, which I knew they wanted. I said I'd have a word with the shoremaster and he came to the office. He had all these references, DR, which was 'declined to report', so he was jumping ship and the Dock Board weren't into that at all. He certainly hadn't been a model seaman."

The founder of the Cavern, **Alan Sytner (100)**, recalls, "When I was about 14, I was in a pub where the Merseys were playing. They had a bad-tempered trumpet player called Wally Fisher. At the time, the trad jazz fans were very self-righteous and thought modern jazz was evil. They were zealots in their hatred of this new music and in one of the other bands was a trumpet player with a modern-looking trumpet playing modern jazz. Wally was so upset that he nutted him and the trumpet player was Ross McManus, who is Elvis Costello's father."

Frank Robinson (101): "That's certainly true. Wally got into an argument with him in the toilets of the Tudor Room about whose music was the best and he head-butted him. Wally was a rough diamond and he had done time for stealing motorbikes."

Ross McManus (102): "It wasn't really a fight at all. There was no bad blood between Wally and me as I hardly knew him. I knew he played the trumpet but he was in the trad group and I played modern jazz and so we wouldn't admire each other's playing in any way. I was playing at a club in some luxury hotel in Liverpool. A group of people wanted me to play and they were badgering Wally to lend me his trumpet. Instead of giving it to me, he suddenly butted me in the face. He was just exasperated. I never saw him again and I never held any grudge against him because, in a way, his action was justified. Everyone was saying, 'Lend Ross your trumpet' and he didn't want to. But it wasn't a fight. I'm a lover, not a fighter."

Ken Baldwin (103): "Wally wasn't sacked, he just left. A year had gone by and it was obvious that he wasn't going to make it as a jazz musician. We only had six numbers and three of them were 12-bar blues and we wanted to move on."

John Lawrence (104): "Wally didn't just leave the band: he left

Liverpool as he wanted to get away from his wife. Years later, we were playing at the Sportsman and Wally turned up and sat in with us. He'd had a few and he wasn't very good. He had a very fiery, forceful approach to the music. He would go at 'Tiger Rag' and 'Dr Jazz' like a bull at a gate. It came off but he was never a polished performer." Wally Fisher played with country bands in his later years: in the 1980s he sat in with Joe Rogers at the Goat in Great Howard Street, at first playing trumpet on his Mexican songs but then playing on everything. For several years, he was with Sonny Phillips' country band where he was known as 'Wally the Bugle'. When he was dying in August 1997, his main concern was for the welfare of his 14 cats.

Sonny Phillips (105): "I met Wally Fisher about 25 years ago and he played trumpet in my country band. We did a show with Paddy Kelly, the Hillsiders and a couple of other bands at the Queen's Hall in Widnes in 1976 and the promoter, Fred Bowler, was setting up the stage. He assumed Wally played the steel guitar and told him where to sit. When the show started, Wally came on with his trumpet behind his back and Fred got a shock when Wally started blowing. He said, 'We can't have that on a country show', but I said, 'Why not? There are trumpets on some of Johnny Cash's records and Marty Robbins' and Tom T. Hall's.' When we did 'Ring Of Fire', he didn't play the trumpet part - our guitarist did that - he had his own ideas and played the trumpet like a steel guitar. He could blow in any key and he liked throwing in other tunes - for the second break in 'Folsom Prison Blues', he'd play 'The Sheik Of Araby' and he'd put 'Colonel Bogey' into 'Throw Another Log On The Fire'. He put some jazz riffs into that Kris Kristofferson song, 'Loving Her Was Easier'. I remember Andy Harris asked Wally to play on a show once and they were going to play 'Baker Street'. Wally had had a extra large spliff that night and when Andy announced 'Baker Street', he went into 'Coronation Street' instead, which the audience thought was very funny. No matter where he was, he always came up with the goods. He was a tough character. He had an argument over money in the Green Man with a bass player and even though he was in his sixties, he smacked this guy so hard that he fell back ten feet. When the bass player's son came to collect him, he started up again and Wally hit him again. Another time he sold a set of drums for £150 and the feller paid him a deposit of £20 and then collected the drums behind his

59

back. Wally didn't see him for a few years and then one night we were playing in a pub in Skem. When Wally took a solo, he would close one eye and it was like he was staring at you. In this case, he was staring at the feller selling socks and shorts as it was the same person. He went white when he saw Wally who demanded his money. He said he hadn't got it and Wally said, 'Then I'll take what you've got, and I'll have your socks and shorts too.'"

Wally Fisher notwithstanding, the Merseys, on the whole, have had strong support for what they were doing. **Don Lydiatt (106)**: "I got married the same year that I joined the band, 1949. My wife was keen on jazz too, but it wore off after a few years! I've two children and although my son has his own business in sound engineering, neither of them has shown much interest in playing an instrument."

Frank Robinson (107): "I got married in 1950. My wife was not into jazz but she always went along with it and never stopped me from playing. I've two boys and four grandchildren, but there isn't a musician amongst them, more's the pity."

Over 50 years on, **Dennis Gracey (108)** is sorry to have left the MJB. "I left the band because I met a young lady, fell in love and that took priority over the music. I don't regret getting married but I regret letting the band down as I did."

John Lawrence (109): "Dennis Gracey left the band to get married as his fiancée didn't think it was a very good idea to have him playing in the band. Subsequently, he got divorced so he might just as well have stayed in the band! He got married again and is now very happy as he has taken up jazz all over again." By way of contrast, the Mersey's first drummer, Ken Metcalfe, left in 1950 because his daytime job involved considerable travelling and he never played again

Frank Parr (110): "I decided to play in 1950. The original band was losing two players, Wally Fisher and Dennis Gracey, and so my friend John Lawrence and myself went out and bought our instruments, cornet and trombone respectively, on the same day. I remember getting home and thinking, 'My god, what have I spent £13 on?' as that was a lot of money then. I had a couple of lessons from Tom Rigley, who was the principal trombone player for the

Phil and enjoyed jazz himself. Fortunately, John and I picked up our instruments pretty quickly and got into the band."

John Lawrence (111): "The trumpet player and the trombone player had both left unexpectedly and Dick Goodwin was stuck for people to replace them. Frank Parr and I were the number one fans of the band - we'd been just about the only fans at one time - and we were asked to have a go. Neither of us had played instruments before, but I bought a cornet for £6 and Frank bought a trombone for a little bit more and we started making the most appalling noises. Eventually it started to take shape."

Frank Parr and John Lawrence joined the Merseysippi Jazz Band in April 1950 and had their first outing at the Mayfair Restaurant in Lime Street three months later. They knew they would have to get themselves into shape for an important concert in Harrogate with the Saints Jazz Band and the Yorkshire Jazz Band to commemorate the Battle of Britain. **John Lawrence (112)**: "We were booked for that concert in September 1950 and we thought we'd better get in a lead trumpet player as I might not have got the hang of it by then. Dick spoke to Bob Crossley from Southport about joining the band. I don't think that he was all that keen and as the concert approached, he said that he wasn't able to join. So the refurbished Merseys were left with two members who could hardly play. We couldn't get out of the engagement but we got by all right as we didn't have to do a lot. One of our new tunes was 'Milenburg Joys'. We had worked out an arrangement and as we weren't all that good at remembering arrangements, we took a wind-up gramophone to Harrogate and played the Lu Watters record in the dressing-room before we went on stage."

Jazz Band Ball Ticket, 1949

(Left to right, top row) Sinclair Traill (editor of 'Jazz Journal', Brian Horrocks (Wallasey Rhythm Club), Dick Goodwin, Ken Metcalf, unknown tuba player, Frank Robinson
(Left to right, front row) Dennis Gracey, Wally Fisher, Pat Evans, Nob Baldwin

Ormskirk Carnival

JAZZ AT THE TOWER

THIRD CONCERT —— NEXT SUNDAY, 11th JUNE.
B.B.C. JAZZ CLUB'S FAMOUS

FREDDY RANDALL

AND HIS BAND.

with

JUNE RAMAR

and featuring

NORMAN CAVE and GENE COTTRELL
(late of the Liverpool Jazz Club).

FOURTH CONCERT —— SUNDAY, 18th JUNE.

Britain's Representatives at the Dutch
Jazz Festival.

MICK MULLIGAN

AND HIS MAGNOLIA JAZZ BAND.
With GEORGE MELLY.

Tickets - - 2/-, 3/-, 4/-.

There is a great demand for tickets for all these shows
and very early booking is recommended at Rushworth &
Dreaper, Liverpool, Birkenhead and Chester; or at
Chesters Ltd., 139, Victoria Road, New Brighton; or at
R. A. Strother & Sons Ltd., 8, Seaview Road, Wallasey.

HAROLD and ALBERT
ROSEN KINDER
of the
LIVERPOOL JAZZ CLUB
present

JAZZ at the TOWER
(SECOND CONCERT)

.. A JAZZ ..
JAMBOREE

GEOFF LOVE
MERSEYSIPPI
JAZZ BAND
YORKSHIRE
JAZZ BAND
SAINTS
JAZZ BAND

TOWER THEATRE
NEW BRIGHTON
SUNDAY, 4TH JUNE
1950.

PROGRAMME — THREEPENCE

Jazz at the Tower

PROGRAMME
(Subject to Alteration).

SAINTS JAZZ BAND.

Georgia Cake-walk.
High Society.
A Closer Walk with Thee.
Baby won't you Please Come Home.
Original Dixieland One-Step.
Smoky Mokes.
Careless Love.
When the Saints.

MERSEYSIPPI JAZZ BAND.

Ding Dong Daddy.
Tin Roof Blues.
Black and Blue.
Joshua Fit de Battle of Jericho.
Canal Street Blues.
Sweet Georgia Brown.
Dippermouth Blues.
Basin Street Blues.

YORKSHIRE JAZZ BAND.

Big Chief Battleaxe.
Doctor Jazz.
Careless Love.
I wish I could Shimmy like my Sister Kate.
Yellow Dog Blues.
Ja Da.
We will walk through the Street of the City.
Get out of Here.

YORKSHIRE JAZZ BAND.
(Yorkshire Jazz Club).

Dickie Hawdon	Cornet	Sleepy Green	Piano
Alan Cooper	Clarinet	Bob Barclay	Tuba
Genius O'Donnell	Trombone	Kit Bell	Banjo
		Arty Mann	Drums

MERSEYSIPPI JAZZ BAND.
(Liverpool Jazz Club).

Wally Fisher	Trumpet	Frank Robinson	Piano
Don. Lydiatt	Clarinet	Dick Goodwin	Bass
Geoff. Love (Guest)	Trombone	Ken. Baldwin	Banjo
		Ken. Metcalfe	Drums

SAINTS JAZZ BAND
(Lancashire Society of Jazz).

Mike McNama	Trumpet	Johnny Fish	Piano
Al Radcliffe	Clarinet	Tommy Gregory	Bass
Ron. " Slim " Simpson	Trombone	Jim Lolly	Banjo
		John Mills	Drums

MERSEYSIDE FESTIVAL OF JAZZ FIXED FOR APRIL

CONTINGENTS of jazz fans from all parts of the North-West are expected to flood the 3,600-seater Liverpool Stadium on Sunday evening, April 2, for the first Merseyside Festival of Jazz. Top-line outfits already booked for the three-hour show, which will begin at 6.30 p.m., are Freddy Randall and his Band, Ralph Sharon and his Sextet, and Kathleen Stobart and her New Music.

They will be supported by Mick Mulligan and his Magnolia Jazz Band, the Terry Walsh Bop Group, the Tommy Smith Swing Group (both from the Hot Club of Liverpool), and the Merseysippi Jazz Band (resident at Liverpool Jazz Club).

The organisers—concert promoters Kenro Productions—promise at least a forty-minute session from the main music groups. Two special band-stands will be built for the festival which is being staged as part of the Liverpool Personal Service Society's £10,000 appeal campaign.

Said the organisers, "It will be the biggest of its kind that Merseyside has seen. The only musical function previously staged on such a scale has been the MELODY MAKER All-Britain Dance Band Championship."

Tickets at prices ranging from 2s. to 7s. 6d. and 10s. may be purchased from the sole ticket agency. Rushworth and Dreaper's, Islington, Liverpool.

LIVERPOOL
JAZZ CLUB NEWS
OCTOBER, 1950.

MONDAY and FRIDAY JAZZ

WELCOME to all Merseyside Jazz Fans will be the news that the LIVERPOOL JAZZ CLUB is re-opening in two sections.

Memories of last season at the Tudor with two groups clamouring for different types of music not to forget quite a few individuals who wanted to hear both types led to this wise (we hope) decision.

Membership of the LIVERPOOL JAZZ CLUB allows entry both clubs and we ask you to please complete the form below and forward it with this year's subs of 2/6 to the Club Secretary, 7, Penrydd Way, Liverpool, 6, as quickly as possible as NO JOINING AT THE DOOR WILL BE ALLOWED AT EITHER CLUB AND NO PERSON WILL BE ALLOWED IN UNLESS THEY HAVE A CURRENT MEMBERSHIP CARD WITH THEM.

FREDDY RANDALL AND HIS BAND make a Special Flying VISIT to the Picton Hall on Sunday, 12th November.

Tickets at usual prices from RUSHWORTH'S. This concert has been arranged by KENRO PRODUCTIONS.

SPECIAL REQUEST VISIT BY HUMPHREY

Booking has commenced at Rushworth & Dreaper's and at Hessy's for the requested welcome return visit of HUMPHREY LYTTELTON AND His BAND at the Picton Hall on Sunday, 5th November.

The concert commences at 7-30 p.m.

PICK-A-TUNE COMPETITION

The competition to select the six tunes people most want to hear played by Humphrey Lyttelton on 5th November, resulted in the following tunes being selected:—Muskrat Ramble, High Society, At the Jazz Band Ball, That's a Plenty, When the Saints and Royal Garden Blues. The nearest sel-ction to these were made by Mr. B. Hall of 6, Ingleton Road, Liverpool, 18 and Mr. F. Matthews of 63, Inward Road, Liverpool 19.

Each will receive an autographed record from Humphrey at the 5th November concert.

OLIVER to TRISTANO

NEW ORLEANS

The New Orleans Club holds its opening session at the well known MAYFAIR RESTAURANT in LIME STREET on Monday, 30th October at 7-30 p.m. and sessions will be at the same time every Monday night. In attendance will be a rejuvenated, resuscitated MERSEYSIPPI JAZZ BAND and there should be no complaints when they play in the new season. It is also intended to present some new and exciting groups at the Club.

MODERN MUSIC

Ross McMANUS, who we can truthfully say led the most popular of any modern group heard at the Club last season, is to lead the resident group at the Modern Music Club. With his trumpet and GEORGE CARROLL's inspiring tenor, backed by an impressive rhythm section we expect some solid sounds to emanate from the CASTLE RESTAURANT in Dale Street every Friday night from 7-0 p.m. when the Club is in session. Opening night will be Friday, 10th November and since space is very limited you are are advised to put in an early appearance to avoid disappointment.

JAZZ MEN WANTED

New Orleans trumpet, clarinet and tuba—details to Club Secretary.

Application For Membership Of Liverpool Jazz Club.

To The Secretary,
    7, Penrydd Way,
        Liverpool, 6.

I apply for membership of the LIVERPOOL JAZZ CLUB and, if elected, agree to abide by the rules of the Club. Enclosed is P.O. value 2/6.

PLEASE USE BLOCK LETTERS

Name ....
                Mr./Mrs./Miss

Address ....

Membership No. last season (where known) ....

Please "cross" P.Os and make payable to "Liverpool Jazz Club."

CHAPTER 4
TEMPLES AND IDOLS
The Temple - Louis Armstrong in Liverpool

I

Fortunately from my point of view, the Merseysippi Jazz Band are hoarders and many contracts, now half a century old, are still around. The band needed no assistance with local bookings but they gave the London-based Lyn Dutton Agency a 10% commission on work outside Lancashire and Cheshire. If you consider that the Beatles, having returned from Hamburg, were only charging £10 a night in 1961, the MJB were very successful. In April 1952 they were booked to appear with Edmundo Ros and his Orchestra at the Winter Gardens, Morecambe and received £50. A contract for them to appear at the Staveley Youth Club outside Nottingham in June 1953 is for £30. It wasn't all mercenary as the Merseys also undertook charity performances.

There are also several tapes of what the band sounded like at the time. **Harold Culling (113)**: "I met my wife in 1951 when I was recording the Merseysippi Jazz Band at a concert in Liverpool, and we have been married 50 years. I had a reel to reel tape recorder from Rushworths in Liverpool. I used to clip my microphone to a stand on the stage and sit backstage and record them. I have kept the recordings. They were more primitive then but they were developing what they are playing today."

When the Merseys went to London on a weekend trip, they crammed in as much as they could. Consider one of the first, in 1951. **John Lawrence (114)**: "We went to London one weekend and we played at the Humphrey Lyttleton club, which is now the 100 Club, and then at Freddy Randall's club at Cook's Ferry. Dick must have approached the BBC as we also went to a BBC studio and played a couple of tunes for an audition."

Don Lydiatt (115): "We failed the audition The producer knew his stuff and said, 'Go and learn your chords and come back when you know what you're doing.' We were buskers at the time, we weren't good musicians."

Frank Robinson (116): "I don't know how Dick had the nerve even to approach the BBC for an audition. The producer told us to organise our chord sequences and that's what we did - the banjo, bass and myself together. By 1952 we had improved immensely and we got a broadcast."

The Merseysippi Jazz Band was booked to give a live concert on the BBC's 'Jazz Club' on 26 January 1952, the same day as a jazz ball at St George's Hall. The local press told how they were going to London and would fly back for the ball, an impressive achievement for the time, but the band realised that this was too much of a risk and persuaded the BBC to record them on location in Liverpool at the Bluecoat Chambers instead. The recording still exists and they performed 'Big Bear Stomp', 'My Journey To The Sky', 'Yellow Dog Blues', 'Snag It', 'Black And Tan Fantasy', 'That Da Da Strain' and 'Chattanooga Stomp'. All they needed to do after the concert was go from School Lane to Lime Street. The following week they were across the road from St George's Hall at the Liverpool Empire with the Squadronaires.

Ken Baldwin (117): "We were picking new numbers by the week and we were rehearsing every Monday night and we soon got our chords sorted. That first broadcast in 1952 from the Bluecoat Chambers wasn't at all bad for the time we'd been together."

Don Lydiatt (118): "The BBC used a landline from the Bluecoat Chambers to London and we were told that it was frightfully expensive. As Lu Watters played in the Dawn Club, we called our first broadcast, 'A Night At The Dawn Club'. It was recorded in the early evening and I can still see the audience sitting in that little room. Afterwards, the compère came over with us to St George's Hall and did the announcements there."

A 25-year-old trumpet player, Pete Daniels, heard the band's first broadcast and had the good sense to record it. **John Lawrence (119)**: "Pete Daniels lived in London and he recorded it from the radio on to acetate discs. He phoned us the next day and told us that he had got the broadcast on record, which was of course very unexpected. He came up and brought the records with him and sat in with the band. We liked him and he liked us and we also liked the bigger sound with two trumpets, so he stayed. He was very easygoing and he thought he would rather have a job in Liverpool and play regularly rather than a job in London and not play very often."

The MJB had the line-up to create the two-horn sound that has been its trademark ever since. **John Lawrence (120)**: "One of the earliest bands was King Oliver's Creole Jazz Band and both Joe Oliver and Louis Armstrong played cornets. In time, cornets gave way to trumpets, but there is not a major difference. We got someone in who happened to be a trumpet player. I happened to play cornet and the two instruments together gave us the sound we wanted."

Kenny Ball (121): "The two trumpet sound derives from the King Oliver Band, although it was probably done by somebody in New Orleans before that. Then it became the Yerba Buena sound and the Merseys took it up. I had the same sound in 1950, 51 as Bill Thompson and myself were both in the Charlie Galbraith Band. As long as the main trumpet player lays down the lead pretty strictly, the second trumpet player, if he has a good ear, follows him, and that is what I used to do with Bill Thompson all the time."

John Lawrence (122): "There is a lot of musical snobbishness. A lot of listeners like what they think is genuine, authentic New Orleans jazz. If you asked them to describe what genuine, authentic New Orleans jazz was, they wouldn't be able to do so. For example, Lu Watters at one time had two banjo players. Nobody else would have thought of copying that, and I don't know why he did it, but if you stray off that line, somebody will criticise you. Now I come to think of it, the Mick Mulligan Band had two banjos at one time, but that was probably because one of them just wasn't loud enough."

From that BBC concert onwards, the MJB acknowledged 'Jazz Club' on their billings. The Merseys played a two hour concert on Sunday afternoon 28 December 1952 at the Tatler Theatre, Chester. The programme lists 26 tunes so the Merseys had a sizeable repertoire by then.

Don Lydiatt (123): "We did have a residency in Lime Street somewhere but the Temple was when things really started to happen. We used to rehearse on Monday nights, sometimes at my house, sometimes at Frank's and sometimes at Ken's. We spread it around a bit to stop the neighbours complaining."

Steve Voce (124): "I looked like an old man when I was quite young so I had no trouble getting into clubs when I was 14. I can remember the Merseysippi Jazz Band playing a place in Lime Street and sharing the bill with a bebop band. In those days, bebop was the antichrist to a trad enthusiast. It was totally unsustainable and unbearable and how they came to pair them together, I don't know. Talk about oil and water - the whole thing was a total disaster."

Still, there were some successful liaisons. **John Lawrence (125)**: "My wife Jasmine also comes from London. She was living in Hounslow and she came here in the early 50s to visit her sister who was at the University. Frank Parr met her and invited her to see the Merseys. She was more interested in modern jazz and she didn't think she would enjoy it. She heard the band and we've been together ever since, getting married in 1961."

II

Chris Barber (126): "Every theatre and cinema was shut on Sunday because of the Lord's Day Observance Society. You could have a live concert, but no fancy dress, costumes or make-up - if you wore a tartan suit, they would close the show immediately. Jazz concerts were a cheap way of doing things, not much paraphernalia and few musicians, so some promoters thought, 'We'll put a lot of amateur bands together, pay them tuppence and call it a Festival of Jazz.' They did it all over the country but the public didn't like it much - there were just one or two good bands amongst a whole lot of rubbish, so it vanished away."

Kenny Ball (127): "In the early 50s, the New Musical Express was owned by a very ambitious man who started a series of jazz concerts at the Royal Albert Hall. There used to be ten jazz bands on each bill and the place would be jumping and heaving. They sent four or five bands round the country and it was the first time I'd left London. Then the hit records started. Ken Colyer was first with 'Isle Of Capri' and then Humph with 'Bad Penny Blues', and this is long before the so-called trad boom. By the time I had a hit in 1961, I was the oldest teenage idol in the business being almost 31."

On 9 January 1955 a concert under the auspices of the National Jazz Federation was staged at the Royal Festival Hall. The night turned out to be a triumph for Ottilie Patterson who was singing with Chris Barber's Jazz Band, but Beryl Bryden also did well, performing with the Merseysippi Jazz Band. Decca released an album from the concert, 'Traditional Jazz Scene, 1955', which included 'Creole Belles' and Beryl's interpretation of Bessie Smith's 'Young Woman's Blues'. 'The Gramophone' commented that Ottilie Patterson "has it all over Beryl Bryden, whose blues sound tired and perfunctory, and most unconvincing, and she takes some pretty big liberties with the lyrics. 'Creole Belles' by the Merseysippi Jazz Band has a Lu Watters sound, good two-beat stuff and a tune that is over 50 years old, but not yet hackneyed. The clarinet is spikey, but the ensemble rides nicely."

John Lawrence (128): "We have never been a big enough name to sell a lot of records through a big company. We worked for a small independent company called Esquire and we made a lot of records for them. Presumably they got their costs back in sales, but it was never a question of getting into the hit parade. The only time we ever made records for a major company was for Decca when we played at the Royal Festival Hall as part of a concert with Chris Barber, Alex Welsh and the Zenith Six, and because Chris Barber's band was on it, it sold very well. That was the night that Ottilie Patterson made her début and did very well. The promoters felt that we also needed a singer for the concert and we were asked to accompany Beryl Bryden, which also went down very well. She was one of the earliest jazz pioneers in this country and she gave the music a great boost. She was also a one-off like George Melly."

Johnny Barnes (129) of the Zenith Six: "Imagine that, our first visit to London and we're playing the Royal Festival Hall - we were terrified. The trombone player walked up to the wrong mike and froze because it wasn't on. I thought, 'Somebody's got to say something', so I walked to the front of the stage and shouted the announcement. You can hear it on the record, this weak little voice with a Manchester accent."

III

In the mid-50s the Merseysippi Jazz Band had a weekly residency at the Temple restaurant in Dale Street in the centre of Liverpool. **Don Lydiatt (130):** "We started off in a room up the stairs at the back of the Temple, and you had to go downstairs to the bar to get a drink and back up again, and 30 people would turn up at first. We decided to knock it off for the summer as the audience would be tailing off, but at the start of June, we suddenly got 40 in and we thought we'd better keep going. Then we reached 50, 80 and 100 people, which was when we moved downstairs. The Temple was tremendous and we used to get 200 people there on a Sunday night. It was a restaurant the rest of the time."

Tommy Hughes (131): "There was a staircase in the Temple that led up to a large room. The sound was incredible for the traditional jazz bands with their trumpets and trombones. The Muskrats used a sousaphone as the bass, which was a heavy piece of pipework wrapped around a feller. If I hear a traditional jazz band today, they don't seem to be loud enough as over the years we have got used to big amplifiers from the rock bands."

Ken Baldwin (132): "We would sometimes play dances where the main attraction would be a dance band with piano, saxophone, bass and drums. The musicians would be reading the scores and there would be a vocalist out front. The dance band would play the first and last set and we would be in the middle. We were enormously loud compared to these other people, but when beat music came in, we were like a whisper because all they had to do was turn a knob."

John Lawrence (133): "The Temple was a venue that we happened to move into when there was nothing else going on in Liverpool, and it was marvellous. We used to play there on a Sunday night and it was the only game in town. Round about five o'clock, a queue used to form and we didn't start until 7.30. They would stand outside in all weathers, waiting to pay half a crown to listen to us. We were the uncrowned kings of jazz music in Liverpool because there was nothing else going on. We would get tremendous crowds and in the end, the management was turning people away. They did very well out of it as the other pubs in Liverpool city centre were deserted on Sunday nights."

Brian Linford (134): "I worked on the door at the Temple and it was a very busy place. There were queues along Dale Street and if you didn't get there by seven o'clock on a Sunday evening, you didn't get in. The Merseysippi Jazz Band was the big attraction in Liverpool as far as jazz was concerned. If you wanted a popular event, then you booked the Merseys."

Ralph Watmough (135): "When Pete Daniels joined the Merseys and they started specialising in King Oliver and Lu Watters, I realised that they were very good indeed. I used to go every Sunday night to hear them at the Temple Restaurant in Dale Street. They had a faithful crowd who filled the place to capacity. When they moved to a bigger room in the same premises, they could get in over 200."

Pianist **Frank Robinson (136)**: "The queues got so big at the Temple that they put a commissionaire on the door. He was very strict about who he let in and on a couple of occasions he wouldn't let me through because I didn't carry an instrument. I had to send for Dick Goodwin to verify who I was. The Temple was a very good place and I never saw any trouble there."

John McCormick (137): "I saw the Merseys for the first time at the Temple. I was only 15 but I managed to sneak in and I was hooked. I thought they were fantastic and I went to see them whenever I could."

Tony Barrow (138): "To me, the Merseysippi Jazz Band was Mersey Beat. It was the music of my generation - it was the band we went to worship in the Temple Restaurant every Sunday night."

Dave Williams (139): "From 1953 to 1955 I was stationed with the RAF in Anglesey. There were lots of Liverpool and Manchester guys on the station and I organised a coach to Liverpool every second week. We went home on Saturday afternoon and returned at midnight on Sunday so I would be in town on Sunday evening and would go to the Temple. I was only 18 and, as there were no clubs open to the general public, it felt racey to go there."

Brian Linford (140): "I've known the Merseysippi Jazz Band since 1953. I knew George Bennett, their drummer at the time, and he wanted help carrying his drums. He travelled by public transport and that meant travelling from Aigburth to the city centre on the 33 tram. After finishing at the Temple, we would go for coffee at the Pier Head. We took the tram to the Pier Head and there was George and myself with his drums and Dick with his bass which was bigger than himself. We would have coffee there and disperse about a quarter to twelve to get the last bus or ferry. Four of the band lived on the Wirral then."

John Lawrence (141): "The trams were the same at each end so you got on at the back end of the tram and the front end by the driver was on the opposite side. Dick Goodwin would wait at a tram-stop with his double-bass and when it came along, he would rush round to the front and ask the driver if he would take it on board alongside him. He would tip the driver but now and again he would get refused. There was a hazard in doing this because the tracks were close together and when two trams passed each other, there was very little space between them, and that space was sometimes taken up by Dick Goodwin and his double-bass. He was trying to get on one tram before the other crushed the bass to matchwood."

There have been more changes among the drummers in the Merseysippi Jazz Band than any other position. (I reckon it's because playing the drums is such a thankless task: if you play clarinet, you can just pop it in its case and go home.) So, by 1954, their third drummer was leaving. **Trevor Carlisle (142)**: "George Bennett, the drummer with the Merseys, had an offer from somebody who offered him more money and he decided to take it. I'd already done a dep with the band and I'd been on the same show with them as part of the Muskrats and they asked if I would be interested in playing with them. I was totally bowled over by it because it was the No I band in the North without any doubt. I had depped with them on an out of town job and maybe that was the audition. They had probably thought, 'Well, he can only get better.' The first night was upstairs at the Temple in Dale Street and it was packed with enthusiasts and it was terrific."

72

Alan Sytner (143): "It wasn't only the Merseysippi Jazz Band who performed at the Temple. They had their own West Coast Jazz Club on Sunday nights and sometimes they booked out of town bands to play there. There was also the Muskrat Jazzmen who played there on Friday nights. It was quite a place for trad jazz, but to be honest, I didn't like trad much. I did when I was young, but by 1956, I was well and truly into modern jazz." By that time, Alan Sytner was all of 21 and ready to make a move that would change the whole perception of Liverpool.

Derek Guyler was a Liverpool actor, who had played washboard in a band called the Washboard Seven whilst at Liverpool College. By 1954 he had established himself as a comic actor but he sometimes sat in with jazz bands on washboard. He responded to a letter of Dick Goodwin's following an appearance on 'Variety Playhouse': "I am afraid that I had to commercialise my performance on the washboard a little in order to amuse the audience. I don't often have the opportunity of using the old board in the traditional style." He accepted the presidency of the West Coast Jazz Club. The letters on file include apologies for not making the club, although he refers to appearing with the Yorkshire Jazz Club, where he was a life member.

The Merseysippi Jazz Band provided the musical Entertainment for stock car racing at Stanley Stadium on 18 June 1954. **John Lawrence (144)**: "The promoters wanted a band to play in the central area of the stadium, but as we were only eight piece, they didn't think that we would make enough noise. They wanted a 15 piece band which they thought would reach the crowds. We brought in our friends from other bands but we were still one short. We had three trombones and they wanted four, but a great drinking friend of ours told us that he had a trombone at home. It had belonged to his grandfather but he couldn't play it himself. He brought it along and mimed all through the performance and got paid his share of the money. It was 30 bob each and they didn't realise that they'd been paying a silent trombone player."

In April 1956 the Merseys' performance at the Temple was recorded by the BBC for a pilot of a radio programme in which three jazz bands in different parts of the country were assessed by a panel of judges. In October 1956, they received a letter from the producer, Richard Kelly, "I am sorry to say that we have had to abandon the scheme for the time being at least. The main reason is that we feel this would have to be a countrywide commitment by the Light Programme in which case it would be a considerable undertaking which they are not prepared for at the moment."

IV

As well as the Temple, the Merseysippi Jazz Band established themselves with concerts about every three months at the Picton Hall in Liverpool. They welcomed and backed Sandy Brown, Beryl Bryden, Dick Hawdon, Cy Laurie, George Melly and Neva Raphaello and played with just about every band of the day including Chris Barber, Ken Colyer, Mike Daniels, Ray Ellington, Terry Lightfoot, Humphrey Lyttelton, Sid Phillips, Alex Welsh, the Christie Brothers Stompers, the Saints Jazz Band and the Yorkshire Jazz Band.

Several American musicians came to Liverpool including Wild Bill Davison and Billy Butterfield and Big Bill Broonzy. Broonzy appeared in concert at the Picton Hall in 1952 and **Frank Robinson (145)** was there: "Big Bill Broonzy was very good but he drank very heavily. He played at the Picton Hall with his acoustic guitar and after every number he picked the wax out of his ears. He didn't have any problems racially in this country or in France, and that is why a lot of the musicians settled there."

In October 1955 he returned to appear with the Merseysippis at the Temple. **John Lawrence (146)** on Big Bill Broonzy: "We thought that we would keep him happy by presenting him with a bottle of Scotch but he had a tremendous thirst and the whole bottle went in no time at all: he was a world class drinker and indestructible. He came from London on the train and when the train pulled into Lime Street, he got out before the train had stopped. He fell and hurt his leg. Pete Daniels introduced him that night as 'Big Bill Bruised Knee'."

Dave Williams (147): "The Temple had a great atmosphere and my most lasting impression is a gig that Big Bill Broonzy did with the Merseysippi. He did a set and then took a break for half an hour. I went to the bar with a couple of friends and Big Bill was sitting at a table. Somebody put a bottle of whisky in front of him with a half-pint tumbler and in the space of 25 minutes, he consumed the whole bottle and then did another absolutely brilliant blues set."

29 June 1952 was to have been a memorable date in the Merseys' calendar as they were to accompany the American singer and blues guitarist, Lonnie Johnson, at the Tivoli Theatre in New Brighton. **Frank Robinson (148)**: "Lonnie Johnson was a wonderful player who had played with Louis Armstrong on some of his records including 'Mahogany Hall Stomp'. He came to Britain but he walked into a union problem as he was barred from playing with British musicians." Thinking on their feet, the promoters booked a singer called Marie Bryant and they did the whole show on their own, two singers and one guitar.

John Lawrence (149): "The Union didn't agree with American musicians coming over here and had this odd theory that it was putting British musicians out of work. I don't know where we could have found a guitar player who could sing and play like Lonnie Johnson but the Musicians' Union didn't see it like that. They could only come if we sent someone in return and who could we send that they would want to listen to? You couldn't expect the Musicians' Union to take a realistic view about anything connected with music, they were more interested in union matters than musical matters. When the American players did come here, they gave additional work to a lot of local players, like us with Louis Armstrong. Every one of his concerts was a gig for an English group."

Couldn't the MJB have defied the Musicians' Union? After all, this wasn't their livelihood but their hobby. **Frank Robinson (150)**: "We have been in the union since 1951 and we had no choice because it was a closed shop. We had to be in the union as we could not have broadcast otherwise, and the union was very strict. We were not allowed to play with other musicians unless they were in the union. We would get a list every month of people who had been blacklisted."

Many of the city's jazz concerts were promoted by Harold Rosen and Albert Kinder, who had met in 1949 and were both involved with the reconstitution of the Territorial Army. **Harold Rosen (151)**: "Louis Armstrong came to Europe and because of the MU ban, we had been plotting to charter a ship and do a concert outside the three-mile limit, but it never came together. I left Liverpool in 1953 and we had promoted a couple of American names - Burl Ives, not too successfully, and Josh White, who went over so well."

In 1955 three of the MJB went to Paris. **Ken Baldwin (152)**: "The union wouldn't allow Louis Armstrong's band over here unless a British band could reciprocate by playing in the States. When we heard they were in Paris, John Lawrence, Frank Parr and myself decided to go over. We got there on Friday afternoon and we went straight to the Olympia and booked for every performance. We saw him twice on Friday, three times on Saturday and twice on Sunday, seven programmes in three days, and we also saw Bill Coleman, another American trumpeter who was playing in Paris. Louis was absolutely marvellous. I remember hearing 'When It's Sleepy Time Down South' as the curtain was rising. I knew his records but to see him in the flesh was fantastic."

John Higham (153): "I saw Louis Armstrong in Hanover when I was stationed there in the army. He played in a huge stadium and everyone was rabbitting away. Nobody was on the stage and then from way out at the back, we heard Louis warming up with 'Secret Love' in a high register and the whole hall went silent"

Frank Parr (154): "The MU ruling was absolutely absurd but eventually reason came to bear. It got knocked on the head and the first American band to appear here was the Louis Armstrong All Stars at the Empress Hall in London in 1956."

Don Lydiatt (155): "When I was on the 'Illustrious', a Canadian had some records by Eddie Condon. They had a very impressive clarinet player called Edmond Hall and I wanted to play like him. When we went to Manchester to see Louis Armstrong and his All Stars, he was in the band. They were coming to Liverpool to fly to Ireland from Speke. Edmond Hall was with his wife so I took them home, got my wife out of bed, and we all became friends. I asked him how he played certain of the tunes and he said, 'Simple'. It may have been simple to him but it certainly wasn't to me."

The Merseysippi Jazz Band was booked as the support act for Louis' concert at the Liverpool Stadium. **Trevor Carlisle (156)**: "The whole band went to see him at Belle Vue in Manchester the week before. Louis did two houses and we went to the second , but as we were waiting outside for the place to empty, we heard his last number, 'The Saints'. That was my introduction to a live American band and it was very emotional. Seeing him was one of the highlights of my life, let alone the thought of appearing on the same bill with him a few days later."

Frank Robinson (157): "The concert with Louis Armstrong at the Stadium in 1956 was our greatest moment. He was a lovely man and very modest in his approach to us, although we must have been hicks to him. There were a lot of photographers around and one lad was having trouble as his flash wouldn't work. Doc Pugh, who toured with Armstrong, said, 'Everybody out', but Louis said, 'No, this cat hasn't had any snaps', and they called him back and let him take what he wanted."

Trevor Carlisle (158): "Being in the same place as Louis Armstrong is one of the greatest things I can think of. Louis and I shook hands and he said, 'Great to see you, man.' I was introduced to his drummer Barrett Deems. Barrett wanted me to use his drum-kit, which was a most fabulous American kit. All drummers wanted to play American drums but I had never played a kit of anything like that standard before. I was worried as to whether I would be able to play it, but I managed okay."

Steve Voce (159): "Louis Armstrong played at the Stadium on a revolving stage. I was a steward and that was absolutely marvellous. Apart from getting in for nothing, I was able to walk round as the stage revolved. I had Louis' trumpet facing me the whole time and I was the only person in the whole stadium who could say that."

John McCormick (160): "I was 16 and that concert was absolutely mindblowing. The anticipation was almost as good as the show. Louis was marvellous and the whole band was fantastic. They gave 110% but Louis even did that in rehearsals. The Merseys must have been nervous but they didn't show it. To be a support for Louis Armstrong is pressure enough but to be a trumpet player is even worse. In fact, their adrenalin was buzzing and they were really hot."

John Lawrence (161): "There was a big revolving stage, which was rather daunting as I could see the audience sweeping past me as I was playing. At the end of the concert, Louis called us on to the stage to play the final tune with him. It was 'The Saints' which is how most concerts ended in those days. Unfortunately, he played in G and we played in F so a lot of miming went on but since he was playing there was no need for us to interfere. We stood around looking hopeful and pretending to play. My most treasured photograph came right at the end of the concert where on the left you can see me playing and on the right you can see Louis with his trumpet held down, so it looks as if Louis Armstrong is listening to John Lawrence, big deal. What happened was, we played 'The Saints', and Louis snapped, 'National Anthem', and stood there. Either he didn't know 'God Save The Queen' or didn't feel inclined to play it, so we played a few bars of it."

The reviewer in the Liverpool Daily Post, whilst acknowledging Louis' talent, was bored: "In the cause of Art, I sat in the Stadium with several thousand perspiring and yelling teenagers to see what it was all about." Not much, is the conclusion. Who cares? Louis was impressed. **Ken Baldwin (162)**: "After the concert, we got a telegram from Louis Armstrong and it said, 'You guys really can w-h-a-l-e' (sic)."

The floodgates had now opened for American musicians in the UK. Carlo Krahmer, the owner of Esquire Records, wrote to Dick Goodwin on 1 May 1957 about all that was happening in London. He had heard, in quick succession, Count Basie, Gerry Mulligan and George Lewis: "British jazz fans like us cannot complain about the lack of visiting jazzmen in the last few months. I hope it continues in this vein."

Unlike the Merseys with Louis Armstrong, not everyone could take the pressure of supporting a major American star. **Roy Williams (163)**, who played trombone with Eric Batty's Jazz Aces in Manchester, remembers the same tour: "There were a lot of people at King's Hall, Belle Vue for Sidney Bechet's concert and during the second half, he brought on the other bandleaders to play along with him and the band he came with, André Réwéliotty and his Orchestra, for a rousing finale of 'The Saints'. There was Mike Daniels from the Delta Jazzmen, Michael Gracie from the Zenith Six and my bandleader Eric Batty. Eric couldn't play very well, and when Bechet started calling the guys up for a solo, he froze in fear. He didn't know what he had to do and Bechet was signalling 'Come on, come on'. Eric was sweating profusely and in what seemed like an eternity to him, he walked to the centre of the stage where there was a microphone and sang a chorus of 'The Saints'. He sang a bass solo and got away with it. He got the best applause of the evening but it upset him deeply and I was so embarrassed for him. There was a bar under the stage for the artists. I got a large drink down me and about ten minutes later, Eric came in, ashen grey, and it unsettled him so much that he never played again."

Steve Voce (164) recalls the visit of another blues musician, Josh White. "I knew all of Josh White's songs and while he was singing at the Cavern, I had come up with some of the responses and he spotted this and we started talking. I took him to the Press Club and we stayed there until two in the morning. I took him home and I put him in the spare room and went to bed. My wife and children who were asleep didn't know that I had brought him home, but my wife was wakened in the middle of the night by some tremendous coughing. She saw me beside her so she knew it wasn't me. She went out on the landing and turned on the light. There was Josh White stark naked looking for the bathroom."

Other households also had unexpected guests. **Ken Baldwin (165)** idolised Sidney Bechet's band: "André Réwéliotty, the piano player, was with Bechet, and Humph was on the show too. They were staying at the Adelphi and I decided to have a party, so André and the Humph band came back to my house, but not Bechet. He had forbidden them to go out: he wanted them in bed early, ready for the concert the next day. We had some fine parties at my place and it's amazing how indiscreet we were. It was a semi-detached house, and we were playing music at two in the morning. Imagine what the neighbours thought, not to mention my mum upstairs." (Eddie Bernard from Bechet's band created amusement by criticising the bad-tempered Bechet at every opportunity.)

Bob Gough (166): "A wonderful singer called Billy Banks came to the UK. I suppose he had to make a living so he appeared as a black man impersonating Al Jolson at the Pavilion Theatre in Lodge Lane. He came to Ken Baldwin's afterwards and the Merseys were there, playing along with him. They did make a recording together and I have a cassette of that which is among my favourites."

Alf Mellor (167): "Albert Kinder worked for Ribble buses but he always wanted to be an impresario. He had no idea as to which performers would go down well in Liverpool and which wouldn't. The concert with Big Bill Broonzy was by no means full. There was even a disappointing attendance for Louis Armstrong at the Stadium, really because he had over-priced the ringside tickets. The organisers made the bad mistake of asking people at the back to come to the front, thereby annoying those who had paid for their ringside seats. I was glad the Merseys were on the bill as I had followed them for some years. I was impressed whenever they did an original number. 'Merseysippi Rag' had been written by Frank Robinson who was also on the buses and worked for Crosville."

The Australian Graeme Bell Band decided to return to London straight after their concert at the Picton Hall. **John Lawrence (168):** "At the end of the concert we were talking to the band and one of them said, 'Are you coming for the session?', and we said, 'What session? We're finished for the night.' They said, 'We're going back on the night train and we're going to have a session on the platform'. We all went over to Lime Street at 11pm. The carriages were full of people wanting to sleep their way to London. Suddenly, 20 jazz musicians started playing. We didn't play for very long as the station master threatened to call the police, but we did get through a couple of tunes."

V

Trevor Carlisle (169) was a professional drummer: "At the time I joined the Merseys, I was between jobs. I had left one job and by working with the band and doing other gigs as well, I found I could earn more money playing in the evenings than I could earn during the day, so there was no point in getting a day job. It's been going on like that for 40 odd years. I've not made a lot of money, but I've had my moments. I'm amazed that they've managed to do it with their day jobs because we would do jobs which incorporated a lot of travel, going up to Redcar, Birmingham and London. The band travelled very widely all over the place and that shows you how enthusiastic they really are."

Ken Baldwin (170): "I'd go into work at nine o'clock but when you are 21 or 22 you can do that. We used to play in London at the 100 Club and come back and I would be dropped off at the door of the dock office at a quarter to nine - I used to work at the Mersey Docks And Harbour Board - and I would go in carrying my guitar and banjo. I would work through the day and play again at night. There was a lack of sleep, but it didn't bother me at all."

As well as playing trombone, **Frank Parr (171)** played cricket for Lancashire: "I started when I was 15 as a colt and moved my way up to become captain. I was a star schoolboy and I was spotted and asked to go for trials with Lancashire. It was a great honour to be asked. I collected the cigarette cards of famous cricketers and now I was meeting them. My first big match was at Lord's for the RAF against the Navy, and Peter May was playing for the Navy. I enjoyed keeping wicket because you are always in the game and my first victim in First Class Cricket was Colin Cowdrey. I was never a great batsman but I was a useful No.8 or 9 and I got my thirties and forties. These were the days before helmets but the only time I have ever been frightened on a cricket pitch was facing Frank Tyson on a rain-affected wicket with the ball behaving very dangerously. I got on fine with Nigel Howard at Lancashire but then Cyril Washbrook became captain and we never saw eye to eye. We were different generations and he never approved of me playing jazz. However, there weren't too many days when I played til 6.30 and then did a gig, and then it was usually a Saturday with no cricket on Sunday. I did appear for the MCC against Yorkshire, which was an England trial. I had an okay game and I was considered for the West Indies tour of 1953 but Godfrey Evans and Dick Spooner got the nod. It's all water under the bridge now but Washy didn't like me and I was out. I was going to go to Worcestershire because Peter Richardson, the captain, was a great pal of mine. It didn't come to pass and Washy may have blocked it. I was very upset at the time, but it's all buried deep in the past now." Well, perhaps not, there is a picture of Washbrook in Frank's home bearing the caption, "Washbrook is a wanker".

Dave Williams (172): "John Lawrence was a tall, good looking guy, who seemed sophisticated at the time, but Pete Daniels was the one who stood out for me. I also liked Frank Parr, but then I was a cricket fan and he was an icon. His captain, Cyril Washbrook gave the impression of being a martinet and I am sure that he didn't stand any nonsense. He thought that jazz was beyond the pale and it probably was if you were a professional sportsman. Indeed, I don't know of any other professional sportsman who has played in a jazz band at the same time"

I asked **Frank Parr (173)** to recall his greatest moment. "In the Roses match of 1952, we were getting the floor wiped with us by Yorkshire. I went in to bat with an hour to go on the last day and we were fighting for a draw. We got to the last over and there was only one wicket to fall. I was there with Bob Berry, who was the number eleven, and he had to face Freddie Trueman with the new ball. The first two balls went by and then Bob hit a ball into the vacant cover point area. I thought, 'Oh my god, we've got to take a single as I am the senior man here.' We did and then Freddie bowled three balls which all pitched on middle and leg and went down the legside. There's the old line and length for you. I never even had to offer a stroke and the game was drawn."

Unfortunately for Frank, he was bowled bouncers by his own side, namely, Lancashire's captain, Cyril Washbrook. He wanted the wicket-keeper stumping and not stomping. **John Lawrence (174)**: "Frank Parr kept wicket for Lancashire for some years and it wasn't an easy time for him as Cyril Washbrook was a disciplinarian. If Frank turned up with a hangover, it didn't go down well. The England wicket-keeper Godfrey Evans was once asked about up and coming players and he mentioned Frank as being possible England material. He never made it to the England team but he did make it to the Mick Mulligan Band which was probably a lot more fun."

George Melly's hilarious book 'Owning Up', which recounts a jazz musician's existence in the 50s and 60s, describes Frank Parr to perfection. He criticises his personality, his hygiene, his eating habits and, with the words pot, kettle and black springing to mind, his drinking habits. For all that, Frank's only criticism of the Melly book is that he refers to him as a wicket-keeper rather than saying he kept wicket. Frank Parr joined the Mick Mulligan band early in 1956 and never played professional cricket again. Melly writes, "Frank's attitude to clothes, like his attitude to so much else, was to use them to make his personality less easy to accept, as yet another barrier between himself and the others. He would, of course, deny this, and make out that he didn't care, but this simply wasn't true. His clothes were not just shabby or old - they were anti-clothes." Frank remained with Mulligan until 1961 and then deputised in various bands, moving into jazz band management, including Acker Bilk's, in 1964.

THE LIVERPOOL JAZZ CLUB
PRESENTS

A JAZZ BALL

AT
ST. GEORGE'S HALL, LIVERPOOL
ON
Saturday, 26th January, 1952
7-30 to 11-30 p.m.
Featuring
Humphrey Lyttelton, Guest Artist with Chris Barber's New Orleans
Jazz Band. Humphrey Lyttelton Trio. Bayou Jazz Band
The Smoky City Stompers. Derek Atkin's Dixielanders
and
The Merseysippi Jazz Band, who are flying back from their initial
" Jazz Club " Broadcast for this function.

Among the Guest Artists it is hoped to present Beryl Bryden, the noted Blues
Singer. Merton Kaye (ex Harry Gold) Ron Simpson (Saints). &c.

Licensed Bars **ADMISSION 5/-**
Refreshments. *Organised by K-R Promotions Ltd.*

INVITATION
Complimentary Ticket
NOT FOR SALE

The British Broadcasting Corporation

ADMIT ONE
to a broadcast performance of
" JAZZ CLUB "
at the
BLUE COAT CHAMBERS, SCHOOL LANE
LIVERPOOL 1
SATURDAY, 26 JANUARY, 1952, at 5.45 p.m.

Children under 12 not admitted
NO ADMITTANCE AFTER BROADCAST HAS COMMENCED

Empire
LIVERPOOL
(Royal 1555)
EVENINGS at 7-15 Matinees Tuesdays, Wednesdays,
Thursdays and Saturdays at 2-15
TOM ARNOLD'S Grand Comedy Pantomime
" BABES IN THE WOOD "
With Those Great Laughter Raisers
JIMMY JEWEL & BEN WARRISS
ADELE DIXON and Big Cast
HURRY ! HURRY ! HURRY ! Only a few seats left
for Liverpool's Greatest Pantomime
Sunday, Feb. 3 — 7-15 — One Performance Only
TWO BROADCASTING BANDS
THE SQUADRONAIRES
THE MERSEYSIPPI JAZZ BAND
2/- to 5/- — Rushworth and Dreapers: Towns Hessy's: Lewis's,
Liverpool.

Daily Graphic, Monday, February 25, 1952

Tune titles finish the show

DERBY magistrates were asked to licence a "concert of a musical nature" in the corporation's King's Hall on a Sunday.

But when they heard the titles of the tunes to be played at the "concert" they banned it.

The titles? "Send me to the electric chair," "Gimme a pig foot," "When the saints go marching in," and "The bottle is empty."

It was to have been a "jam session" on Sunday, March 23—by Mick Mulligan and his Magnolia Jazz Band and the Merseysippi Jazz Band.

And the magistrates' ban

has angered Derby's jazz fans.

Miss Maureen Crutchley, aged 18, assistant secretary of Derby Jazz Club, said yesterday: "I am furious about it. This shows a bias against jazz music.

"Some of the tunes are adapted from spirituals and so should be suitable for a Sunday."

Mr. A. W. Turnbull, Derby Corporation Entertainment Manager, who made the application, said afterwards: "The titles may sound a bit ghastly, but it is amusement for young people."

*Top row: John Lawrence, Frank Parr, Dick Goodwin
Bottom row: Jasmine Lawrence (John's wife), Pete Daniels,
Ken Baldwin*

*John Lawrence plays while Satchmo listens. Velma Middleton is in
front of John*

The Mississippi Boys
They really Can Whale
Best Wishes
Louis Armstrong
Satchmo

CHAPTER 5
UNDERGROUND MOVEMENT
The Cavern - Clinton Ford

I

Alan Sytner (175): "There were no premises dedicated to jazz in Liverpool. It was promoted in pubs, church halls and social clubs, but it was like that all over Britain. The first purpose-built jazz club opened in London in 1956 and that was the Flamingo in Soho. I'd been running little jazz clubs in social clubs to keep my friends happy so that they could have gigs. The Ralph Watmough Band were jolly nice chaps and they asked me if I would help them to run a jazz club. They'd done a gig in a social club in Croxteth Road which had gone down very well. They could have the club on Friday nights for £3, but they couldn't organise it themselves. They asked me to run it and pay them a fee. I had just had a £20 bonus as I worked for a firm that paid Easter and Christmas bonuses and the firm had had a good period. I called it the 21 Club as I was 21 and it was at 21 Croxteth Road. I got other bands to play there too and it proved to be very popular, except on very sunny evenings. It wasn't a big room but it was usually chocker."

Alan Sytner was the son of a docklands GP, Joe Sytner. Joe wanted his son to follow him into the medical profession, but his earlier generosity prevented it. He had effected an insurance policy for Alan when he was a child and it matured when he was 21, giving him £400. **Alan Sytner (176)**: "I was doing okay with the 21 and enjoyed it but I realised that if I had a better place, a more interesting place, I could open two or three or four nights a week, perhaps for different sorts of jazz including modern jazz. I realised that if I rented a property, it would be far more economic per night, and I would have my own say as to when I opened and what I did, so I went out looking for a property that could be turned into a jazz club. I looked at lots of them but nothing was of any great interest."

Alan Sytner (177) had an idea of what he was looking for: "I had spent most of my school holidays in France, and I had spent most of that time in Paris, so that I could go to jazz clubs and see the bohemian life. I was only a kid, 14, when I first went, but I was dazzled by it and it was all part of the glamour of Paris after the war. They enjoyed listening to jazz in Paris, which dates back to the 1920s, and they liked real music and not muzak. Even today the background music in a supermarket could be Charlie Parker or Dexter Gordon."

Mathew Street is just off Liverpool's city centre, but no shopper would have gone there in the 1950s. The narrow street was little more than two rows of seven-storey warehouses, and lorry-loads of fruit and vegetables were being unloaded throughout the day. 10 Mathew Street was typical: the basement had been an air-raid shelter during the war and was later used for storing wines and spirits and then as an egg-packing station. In 1956 the building was being used to store electrical goods, but the basement was vacant. **Alan Sytner (178)**: "An estate agent, Glyn Evans, told me he knew of an old cellar which was full of arches and derelict. I got the keys and went down a rickety ladder with a flashlight. Glyn Evans didn't realise that he was showing me a replica of Le Caveau and that is where the name came from. Mathew Street looked like a little narrow street in the Latin Quarter in Paris, so I felt I was bringing the Left Bank to Liverpool."

The first job was to clear out the site and he recruited many volunteers. An architect friend, **Keith Hemmings (179)**, helped out. "I was a very good friend of Alan's and we used to go on holiday together. He had this great idea of having a jazz club in Liverpool and he found the place and I was going to be his partner. I drew up the plans and with a few friends, we knocked the walls down, put toilets in and built the stage."

Alan Sytner (180): "The place had been reinforced to make an air-raid shelter and the brick reinforcements had to be removed with sledgehammers as we couldn't get a pneumatic drill in. Well, we didn't even know where to get one. We did it by hand and we were left with a lot of rubble. That was the ideal foundation for the stage, which was made of wood and just went over the bricks. It did a great job of balancing the acoustics, and the acoustics in the Cavern were terrific, absolutely brilliant."

Meanwhile, the Merseysippi Jazz Band were growing disillusioned with the Temple. **John Lawrence (181)**: "The licensee, realising that he was on to a very good thing, decided to charge us a lot of money for the room. We were rather annoyed and moved to the Cavern. The Cavern was opened by Alan Sytner, who had found this dirty old cellar in Mathew Street. I was going to say he decorated it, but that would be an overstatement. It was rough and scruffy but it had atmosphere."

In the Merseys' files is a solicitor's letter dated August 1956 which proposes to transfer the ownership of the West Coast Jazz Club to Alan Sytner. An agreement was drawn up together with a separate service agreement for the band's services. Dick Goodwin was a stickler for formality and perhaps he was trying to protect the MJB's bookings. The West Coast Jazz Club would transfer to the Cavern and Alan Sytner would be legally bound to book the Merseys as the resident band. It is far removed from the rough and ready world of beat club bookings a few years later.

First, the Cavern had to open. **Alan Sytner (182)**: "I didn't like rock'n'roll but the initial plan was to launch Bill Haley and his Comets at the Cavern. They were coming over on a boat and the 'Daily Mirror' thought it would be a good idea if their first appearance was at the Cavern. It was a mad scheme that never happened. There would have been no point in putting on rock'n'roll at the Cavern. There were no local bands to speak of and hardly any in London. Tony Crombie, who was a good jazz drummer, formed a rock'n'roll group in order to make some money, but I saw them at the Pavilion and they were awful."

Missing the Christmas and New Year trade, the Cavern opened on 16 January 1957. The opening bill featured the Merseysippi Jazz Band, the Wall City Jazzmen, the Ralph Watmough Jazz Band and the Coney Island Skiffle Group. The guest of honour was to be the 21 year old drummer, the Earl of Wharncliffe. **Bob Azurdia (183)**: "The queue stretched all the way down Mathew Street and into Whitechapel. Prior to the Cavern, the Temple was the only evening venue for jazz in the city and it opened only on Sunday nights. Life was very different in those days. The only other places you could go to were a cinema, a palais for strict-tempo dancing or a coffee bar. Young people tended not to go to pubs, which in any case closed at ten without any drinking-up time. The Cavern was therefore very welcome."

The doorway was lit by a single bulb. 18 stone steps led down to the cellar which was divided by archways into three long, dimly-lit barrel vaults, each a hundred feet long and ten feet wide. The walls were painted plainly with emulsion and there were no curtains or decorations. The entrance to the first vault was used to collect admission money and there was also a cloakroom. The second and largest area contained the stage and a few rows of wooden chairs. All the lighting (no coloured filters or bulbs) was concentrated on the stage. There was only dancing - the Cavern stomp - when there was room to move. It was an excellent arrangement, but the lavatories were appalling, the bandroom tiny and the air-conditioning non-existent. Most people smoked and within minutes of opening, the Cavern could contain hundreds of sweaty bodies. Condensation would cover the walls and drip off the ceilings.

Intriguingly, **Alan Sytner (184)** decided against a liquor licence for the Cavern. "I wasn't anti-booze but my heart wasn't in it and I didn't think that I could meet the requirements for a liquor licence. I was going to get a lot of young people in the place and so it wasn't a good idea to have booze there. They could always get a passout and go to the White Star or the Grapes, where incidentally they might find me."

Many Beatle books have them entertaining them up to 1,100 fans at the Cavern but that is an impossibility. **Alan Sytner (185)**: "The maximum ticket sale that we had was 652, and that was on the opening night where we turned more away than we let in. Only a third of the people got in. We had mounted police to control the queue which stretched for half a mile, but, unlike today, there was no trouble when they told people to go home. We got very close to 652 on several other occasions, but it got very heavy when it got to 600. It is also good to say 'Sorry, we're full' when you're in the entertainment business. We didn't get to 600 that often, but when we did, we would say, 'That's enough'."

Don Lydiatt (186): "I remember walking up Whitechapel to the Cavern and I was walking alongside the queue. It was obvious that it was going to be full, but it was very odd that the Earl of Wharncliffe didn't turn up."

I wondered what the Earl of Wharncliffe was doing on the bill for that opening night. **Alan Sytner (187)**: "The Earl of Wharncliffe had nothing whatever to do with jazz or blues: he had a very iffy rock'n'roll band which only got PR because he was an earl. However, I was keen to make an impact and there was a jazz promoter in Liverpool who had a monopoly on the main jazz bands so I couldn't hire any. I couldn't get Chris Barber, Ken Colyer or Humphrey Lyttelton for the opening and I had to do something to make some impact. I was a member of Liverpool Press Club and one of the boys suggested the Earl of Wharncliffe and said they would do a story about it. In the end, he didn't show up because he was at Cirencester Agricultural College and he'd had an ultimatum - Stop doing gigs and go back to college or get expelled. He was hauled back but he didn't bother to inform me. Eventually I got a call when everybody was in the club. I had to announce that he wasn't coming, but nobody was the least bit bothered because having got into the Cavern on the opening night, everybody was thrilled to be there. We had lots of good bands on and everybody had a great time. The fact that the Earl never showed was much better than if he had. He did gigs all over the place so his not showing was a national story."

Ralph Watmough (188): "We played on the opening night of the Cavern. The Cavern was an old bonded warehouse and someone had limewashed the walls. The unexpected din from the musicians caused the limewash to flake off. The Wall City Jazz Band from Chester played the first set and they came off looking like snowmen. They were covered from head to foot and Alan Sytner had to do something to stop it happening again. The Cavern must have been a fire officer's nightmare. There was only one entrance and exit down a very narrow steep flight of steps. There were no toilets to speak of and a club like that could never exist these days."

Roger Baskerfield (189) of the Coney Island Skiffle Group: "I played here on the first night. I was also here when Lonnie Donegan came down to have a look at his skiffle club one lunchtime. Before Lonnie came on the scene, everybody used to listen to music. When Lonnie came around, everybody bought a guitar and everybody played music It was so hot on the opening night that I fainted in the dressing room. When I opened my eyes, I found four girls undoing my shirt, so I quickly closed them again."

Keith Hemmings (190): "Right from the first night, I knew the Cavern was going to be a tremendous success. There was such a spirit in the place - it was so vibrant and exciting. I was going to be Alan's partner, but we fell out and I disappeared from the scene about a fortnight after it opened. I went into the family business and I have forgotten about my involvement with the Cavern, to be honest with you."

John Lawrence (191): "I can't remember what triggered the Cavern's instant success as I can't remember Alan doing a lot of advertising about the Cavern. I thought that we were taking a bit of a chance by moving from a moderately comfortable pub to a damp cellar, but it was the best thing that ever happened to us. They came flooding in every time we played there. The stage was just about big enough for an eight-piece band, but the piano was hanging over the edge. Acoustically it was very good as there were three long tunnels - the outside tunnels were full of benches and chairs and the centre tunnel with the stage at the end was acoustically just right. It was a long room with hard surfaces, brick and a stone floor, which is always good. If you play in a room full of curtains and thick carpets, you can blow your teeth out trying to make the sound right."

Frank Robinson (192): "Quite surprisingly, the piano at the Cavern wasn't all that bad and it was kept in tune. It didn't have a brilliant tone and it was a bit muddy, but it did the job."

Don Lydiatt (193): "We only had one microphone and the amplification wasn't very good anyway. We just blew and hoped for the best. We got used to it."

Steve Voce (194): "Acoustically, the Cavern wasn't brilliant but we were all much younger and our hearing was much more acute. I can't remember any problems in hearing bands there. If you'd had a few pints, it was a good place to hear jazz but then I don't think I ever tried to hear it without having a few pints."

Brian Linford (195): "I preferred to see the Merseys at the Temple than at the Cavern. It had a much greater atmosphere and was full of jazz lovers. Within two years the Cavern sessions had closed and a lot of the real jazz fans had disappeared."

In March 1957 a public health inspector blew up some football bladders at the Cavern to obtain air samples. Outside it was 52 degrees Fahrenheit and inside 82, a remarkable difference when there was no heating in the club. However, the inspector lacked the powers now available to an environmental health officer and could only recommend that the owner should improve his facilities.

What does **Alan Sytner (196)** think of that? Should he have improved conditions at the Cavern? "I didn't have the finances to do that and anyway the places in Paris were pretty stark. I knew that if I fancied it, they would fancy it, simple as that. I was 21, a little more sophisticated than the average Scouse 21 year old, but nonetheless, I was a 21 year old Scouser and I knew that they would like it. The Cavern was bigger than the places I'd seen in Paris, which were also licensed and charged more for admission. Their clubs had an ambience and I knew how to get that at the Cavern."

The Merseysippi Jazz Band played the Cavern five times during the opening month and it quickly established itself as the hippest place on Merseyside, not that there was much competition. **Alan Sytner (197)**: "There were very marked demographics according to the night of the week and what was being put on. On Thursdays I put on modern jazz to please myself and again I got a very hip, very cool audience - crew-cuts, button-down collars and little skinny ties. They thought they were massively superior and cleverer than everybody else. These were people who had their own cars and so we could stay open a little later. Sunday was the Merseys' night and they attracted a very middle class audience with lots of people from the Wirral and Crosby. These people didn't cause any trouble at all, obviously, and as they formed the majority, nobody else did either. Friday night was completely different. We used to get kids from the top end of London Road. There were quite a few gangs and they used to love making trouble, similar to football hooligans today and the same sort of people. If I'd had any sense, I would have closed on Fridays. On Saturdays you got a cross-section. If there was a band with a strong appeal, you would get a nice audience. If it was a so-so band, you would just get whoever was out on Saturday night and going to the Cavern for want of anywhere else to go."

Valerie Dicks (198): "I was a student nurse at Sefton General and I used to wear my uniform on the bus because the bus conductor wouldn't take the fare and I never had enough money to pay the fare anyway. Everybody has somebody who is sick sometime and maybe a nurse looked after your mother or sister, so you didn't charge them. It was a shilling to get in at the Cavern and I would get in for half price because of my uniform. I would go into the toilets and change into my clothes and put my uniform in a bag. The water ran down the walls: you went in with straight hair and you ended up with curls. One side was for those who hadn't done much educationally and the other side was for the ones who went to grammar school, and we kept to our sides. Thelma ran a coffee bar at the top end and would dish out Cokes and hot dogs. When the pop groups came on, who were the fill-ins for the jazz groups, we would go to the White Star or the Grapes with a bottle of Coke from Thelma. We would empty the Coke down the grid and come back with Cherry B and cider in the Coke bottle, drinking it through a straw. Thelma often wondered why we were so happy at the end of the night. I would put my uniform back on and go back home on the bus."

Ken Baldwin (199): "We would go over to the Beaconsfield in the interval and Mr Cosgrove with his steel grey hair was immaculately dressed with a flower in his lapel. The doors would burst open and the whole band would clatter down the steps and Mr Cosgrove would say, 'Jim, the boys', and Jim would start pulling the pints. Mr Cosgrove was in charge and he never pulled a pint himself. Mr Cosgrove knew we played at the Cavern, and every Christmas he would send us a bottle of Scotch, a bottle of gin and a bottle of rum. That was because we used to bring custom into the Beaconsfield."

Alan Sytner (200): "The famous story of Brian Epstein coming down into this murky gloomy place and having his mind blown by the Beatles is absolute crap. He had been to the Cavern lots of times previously. He came down on Sunday nights, he was a very middle-class boy and so were his friends. Brian Epstein asked me to arrange a band for his 21st birthday party, and I told him that the Merseysippi Jazz Band would cost about £25. He asked if there was anything cheaper, and I said, 'Yes, I can get you the Blue Jeans for £12.'"

The Blue Jeans embraced skiffle, jazz and eventually beat music. **Alan Sytner (201)**: "There were hundreds of skiffle and blues groups in the country, the Lonnie Donegan factor was mega, so on Wednesdays I put on a competition for local talent. It encouraged kids who were learning to play, and I would have a couple of more accomplished groups who could play. These kids did the Lonnie Donegan, Dickie Bishop and Johnny Duncan repertoires and they were all pretty awful. Talent night was no talent as far as I was concerned but I wasn't being altruistic as skiffle was very commercial."

Steve Voce (202): "We disliked skiffle with almost the same contempt that we disliked rock'n'roll. I didn't like Lonnie Donegan in the least, but he saw an opening and seized it The only reason that skiffle was tolerated at the Cavern was because it made some money for some jazz musicians whom we were sympathetic to. The genuine skiffle music - Big Bill Broonzy, Blind Lemon Jefferson, the people from the 20s - was marvellous, but the later thing was a fraud."

John Lennon's Quarry Men made their debut at the Cavern on 7 August 1957 and then again on 24 January 1958. **Alan Sytner (203)**: "Skiffle was a breeding ground for musicians - one or two of them became jazz musicians, but more ended up doing rock. Lennon and McCartney were there, I know that because I had a girlfriend at the art college who was in the same class as John, and she persuaded me to let them play and they were diabolical. I knew John Lennon quite well as we lived in the same area: he lived 400 yards up the road from me. They were 16 and arrogant and they hadn't got a clue, but that was John Lennon, and no doubt Paul McCartney caught it from him. John Lennon was considered a huge personality at the art college by all the kids and Ann told me that he would like to play. They'd only been playing for a short while so you wouldn't expect them to be any good but they became world class, the best. At the time, they couldn't play to save their lives and all I can remember is their cheek and their chat."

Colin Hanton (204): "We did some skiffle numbers to start off with but we also did rock'n'roll. John was passed a note and he said to the audience, 'We've had a request'. He opened it up and it was Alan Sytner saying, 'Cut out the bloody rock'n'roll.'"

94

Steve Voce (205): "The jazz that the Cavern put on covered all the extremes. We had Ronnie Scott and Tubby Hayes, where you needed to use your intelligence a bit more and the rewards were substantially greater, while the Merseys were at the banjo end of jazz, the boozing end where you don't have to use your brain. The fact that they have stuck together demonstrates great loyalty or restricted imagination. Don Lydiatt attempted to play like Benny Goodman and John Lawrence was influenced by Shorty Rogers. They didn't slavishly copy the New Orleans music which was out of date by 1929. The banjo was not being used by Johnny Dodds, Kid Ory or Louis Armstrong after 1928, so what the hell are people using it for now? It shows a lack of intelligence."

Alan Sytner (206): "Some of the modern jazz musicians were really laid-back and terribly unpunctual. They took playing seriously but they didn't take making a living seriously. They were all pros, but they were very hard to deal with. Tubby Hayes, the little giant, was the worst. Once he came to Liverpool on the train and he drank 28 bottles of Worthington Green Shield between Euston and Lime Street, but he was all right, he was an amazing bloke, but he wasn't *that* all right. He still played. Another night he turned up at 10 o'clock for an 8 o'clock gig. He was full of apologies and said he would play until one in the morning, knowing full well that we had to close at 11.30."

Steve Voce (207): "Jazz was still being polarised between modern fans and traditional fans, and Ronnie Scott and Tubby Hayes would never have had a platform in Liverpool if it wasn't for Alan Sytner. The barriers broke down when Humphrey Lyttelton dragged them together very slowly by having a band which combined the best aspects of both. Alan Sytner deserves a lot of credit for what he did, but he didn't change the jazz scene like Les Jenkins at the Manchester Sports Guild. He had this marvellous cellar and he would book American acts like Red Allen and Edmond Hall to play there and then find other work for them. This was unique and he and his assistant Betty gave their lives for jazz. The hard work killed him."

The gospel singer Sister Rosetta Tharpe was backed by the

Merseysippi Jazz Band in Manchester and then by the Wall City Jazzmen at Cavern. She voiced her doubts about appearing at the Cavern by saying, "You might wonder what a woman of God like me is doing in a place like this. Well, our Lord Jesus went down into the highways and the byways and if it's good enough for Him, it's good enough for me." By not being licensed, the Cavern was not wayward enough for Tharpe's husband, who was known as Lazy Daddy. **Steve Voce (208)**: "The licensing laws baffled all Americans except Lazy Daddy, who had a complete working knowledge of opening hours within 20 minutes of stepping off the boat."

III

The Merseysippi Jazz Band contained eight members, whose personnel was often changing. **Ray Ennis (209)**: "The Merseys were very good but there were such a lot of them that it was like watching the Hallé Orchestra."

John Parkes (210) recalls his audition in 1957: "Dick Goodwin was the manager of the Merseys and somebody had recommended me. I was playing every night in Artie Williams' 18-piece band in Ellesmere Port and Dick asked me if I would like to join. I had been teaching a trombone player from the Merseys to read music, so I knew they were busy and I wanted to play with them. Dick was very casual and asked me to do an audition at the Cavern, which was on the point of opening. I was very nervous as I hadn't played jazz before except for the occasional solo with the big band. They put all these numbers in front of me and I floundered through them. Dick said, 'I'll take you to the Grapes' and I thought, 'This is it, it'll be "No thanks".' He said, 'I've never heard anything like that - you've never played jazz before and yet you were marvellous.' So I was in."

A more daunting experience occurred a few months later. **John Parkes (211)**: "I remember J.J. Johnson, coming down the Cavern and I said, 'Are you going to play for us, J.J?' and he said, 'That's a thing I never do. I've come to hear you play.' Here's J.J. Johnson, the most famous trombone player in the world, sitting there and nodding approvingly while my nerves are going."

Pete Fryer (212): "I lived in Warrington until I was 15 and played trombone in a brass band. Then I moved to a school in Birkenhead and started getting interested in jazz. I saw the Merseysippi Jazz Band at the Cavern and I thought they were great. I was listening mainly to Johnny Parkes, who was a smashing trombone player. I formed a band with my school mates and we had our first gig at St Stephen's church hall in Prenton in 1960. The Merseysippis were our local idols and I would never have dreamt that I'd be playing with them one day."

Noel Walker's Stompers included Derek Vaux who now plays with the Merseysippis. **Noel Walker (213)**: "We had seen the Merseysippis and we wanted to form our own band. Derek Vaux had been playing tea-chest bass with a skiffle group and we formed the band shortly after I left school. Mike McCombe was the drummer and he also played with the Merseys for a long time. I was the leader because my parents were the only ones who let us use the telephone to get gigs and arrange things. I was a bandleader even though I had never picked up an instrument. It became clear that I would have to be a trombone player if I wanted to play in my own band. The person who owned the Iron Door offered us six gigs if we would help him build his bar, which we did. We became a viable attraction, playing at the Iron Door, the Mardi Gras and the Cavern, and also Fort Perch Rock at New Brighton."

Mike McCombe (214): "I came out of the army in 1959 and I joined Noel Walker's Stompers. We only had a rudimentary knowledge of our instruments and so we were probably pretty bad. We often had gigs at the Student's Union at Liverpool University and there was a big Coca-Cola sign on the wall to the right of the bandstand. One night Noel was all over the place and couldn't find his notes at all. In the interval we asked him what he was doing and he said, 'They've taken the sign down. When the end of my slide is level with the first 'o' in Coca-Cola, I know I'm in B flat. I don't know where I am tonight.'"

Clinton Ford (215), or rather Ian George Stopford Harrison, began life in Salford on 4 November 1931: "I was born in Salford but only because my grandfather couldn't get work on the Liverpool docks. He was a superintendent stevedore and he walked to Salford with his family, pushing my father in a pram. He had no money and he found work when he got there."

Clinton Ford (216) wanted to work as a professional musician: "I was going on tour with a show in 1957 with a group I had formed called the Backwoods Skiffle Group, although it wasn't really skiffle. I thought that my real name didn't sound right and someone came up with Clinton Ford, which fitted in with the Backwoods Skiffle Group much better."

In 1958 **Clinton Ford (217)** worked in Butlin's, Pwllheli as a Red Coat. He would dress in a cowboy outfit and sing western songs, his long, lanky frame working in his favour: "I had family in Bebington but I had never really come to Liverpool until I went to the Cavern. I sang 'Ace In The Hole' with Ralph Watmough and then someone asked if I could sing with the Merseys. Frank Robinson said, 'Not another one', and I've been singing with them on and off ever since. I like the sound they make and they are good to sing with. Most of them do a little vocal or two and they have had permanent singers on and off but I am their longest serving singer even though it is only spasmodic."

Clinton Ford sang with the Merseys for the first time at the Cavern on the night the trams finished in Liverpool. **Frank Robinson (218)**: "I was apprehensive about Clinton because most people who want to sing with the band don't have much idea of keys or intonation. But there was no problem with Clinton, good intonation and good diction, you can understand every word he sings."

Ken Baldwin (219): "We were playing at the Cavern in 1958 and this guy came through the door. It was Clinton Ford but we didn't know him and his face was hidden by a pair of sunglasses. I thought he was a poser - you don't wear sunglasses in a cellar - but there was a reason for this as he had two black eyes. He had just finished a summer season at Butlin's in Pwllheli. He sang in the bar every night and he had become friendly with one of the girls who worked there. He had taken her to his chalet but she happened to be the chef's young lady who sussed out where she was. The chef duffed him up and he still had the shiners when we saw him. He didn't create a good impression at first but as soon as he sang with the band, things were different. We realised he could sing. He knew a few jazz numbers and he had a good voice. His first love was country music which he does very well and then in the nightclubs, he'd be doing 'Fanlight Fanny'. We love playing with him and we know a lot of his numbers."

Noel Walker (220): "Derek Vaux and I were both working in banks which wasn't doing much for our heads at all. We got offered a summer season at Butlin's in Filey and the people in my band didn't want to go with me, apart from Derek, so we formed a new band called the Noel Walker Reverend Jazz Band. Butlin's wasn't moving with the times and we found ourselves playing in a hall, which was named The Rock'n'Calypso Ballroom. The audiences liked trad jazz but the management had no idea how to handle a jazz band. They locked us in at night and we had to crawl across the wire netting to get into our girlfriends' chalets. We kept getting locked out for being drunk, all of the things that normal jazz musicians do. It was most unfair of them to treat us in that way."

Derek Vaux (221) played Butlin's as part of that Reverend Jazz Band: "We got into the same sort of trouble as Clinton really. Clinton told me about the soothing effect singing had on young ladies, especially holidaymakers, and he just had to visit them at three in the morning to console them. At least that was the story he told the camp manager before he was evicted. We were removed from Butlin's for much the same reason but I recall those days with great happiness: it was a time of total irresponsibility and good fun. We did have to suffer various things like the camp padre who insisted on taking the microphone while we were playing because we had packed houses and it was his opportunity to address the holidaymakers. He would start with the words, 'Settle down please and listen to me. I'm one of you, you know, hep cat, go man go.' He used to empty the hall and cause the band members to fall about laughing. The poor fellow never realised how foolish he was making himself, and the pleasure he was giving to us. It also gave us some unexpected time off."

Clinton Ford (222) decided to settle in Liverpool and play with the Merseys when other work, usually at Butlin's, wasn't available. "I had a little bedsit in Canning Street for fifteen shillings a week. It was a marvellous little place. Ron Rubin, who's worked with everyone, had a bedsit opposite to me, but his was smaller than mine and only ten shillings a week. Somehow he got a piano up there. I played my guitar in my room and did write some songs there. I recorded one of them, 'Now That You've Gone'. I liked playing the Cavern with the Merseys but it's hard to convey how squalid it was. When it was packed, the moisture would rise and settle on the ceiling. It would condense and drip down your neck. It was an awful place but we loved it."

Ken Baldwin (223): "Clinton Ford played with us in the wintertime and we learnt a lot of his songs. We were semi-pro and playing three or times a week. We weren't making enough for him to live on, so we knew that he would never stay with us."

Dave Williams (224): "As I was working in North John Street, I used to go to the Cavern at lunchtime and I would often see Clinton Ford with the Merseysippi Jazz Band. More frequently I went on Thursdays to the modern jazz nights to see the likes of Tubby Hayes, Ronnie Scott and Don Rendell. I was miffed when Merseybeat took over and modern jazz nights were discontinued. I felt I was being robbed of one of the few venues in Liverpool that had modern jazz."

John Parkes (225): "You couldn't put Clint in a pigeonhole, but that's one of his strengths. Everybody liked Clint and he always made the night go with a swing. No matter where we were, he would get them eating out of his hand by the end of the evening."

Things certainly could go with a swing with Clinton. **Frank Robinson (226)**: "We were playing at the students' union one night and Clinton noticed a piece of rope that was dangling down backstage. He tied it into a hangman's noose, stood on a chair and put it round his neck. The chair was just a frame and he was stood on the edge. I was telling him not to take any chances when he fell off and I had to catch him quickly."

Tony Davis (227): "I've known Clinton for years and he taught Mick the chords to 'Dirty Old Town' which was our first single in the Spinners. Clint is great fun and very enjoyable but I prefer the Merseys without him. John Barnes is the only man who really adds to the Merseys. When he sits in with them on saxophone, it isn't an eight man band with a guest but a nine man band."

*Dick Goodwin
dressed for manual
labour at the Cavern*

"Best clothes, lads, we're playing the Cavern"

Trevor Carlisle and Dick Goodwin

Humph and Fans

Another wild night for the MJB!

Dancers get oxygen

Ambulance men will stand by at an all-night jazz and bop ball in Leeds on Friday to pep up the flagging dancers with whiffs from oxygen cylinders.

The city's medical officer of health, Professor David Bradshaw, gave the oxygen idea his full approval yesterday. "It will give the dancers a feeling of elation," he said.

Mr Arthur Green, who is organising the dance at the Queen's Hall, said: "We felt that the strain of twisting and bopping all night might be too much for some dancers."

CHAPTER 6
IS THAT YOUR VINYL ANSWER?
Esquire Records

As we have seen, Harold Culling was making private tapes of the Merseysippi Jazz Band from as early as 1951. They made some demonstration records the following year. **John Lawrence (228)**: "There wasn't a lot of polish about the band, but we recorded in the Tick-Tock Café in New Brighton in 1952. It was for Chester's Music Shop in Victoria Street, who used to make private recordings. We just wanted the kick of making a record and we weren't expecting to sell them. It was for our own amusement, which was fairly limited amusement when we heard the playbacks." Also in 1952, they recorded 'Chattanooga Stomp' for the local sound engineer Bernard Whitty, again at the Tick-Tock Café, and this recording also exists.

The first time you could buy a record by the Merseysippi Jazz Band in the shops was a limited edition 78rpm of 'Moose March' and 'Friendless Blues'. This was recorded by Johnny Roadhouse at his Decibel Studios in Manchester, again in 1952. Because of purchase tax restrictions, only 99 copies were pressed. Eight went to the band and the rest were sold commercially. **John Lawrence (229)**: "I am sure it is the first commercially available record by a Liverpool jazz band, but I've no idea how it got set up. Dick always played his cards close to his chest. In 1954 he got in touch with Esquire and said that we were available. Dick, who worked for an accountant, liked to do the organising. He never shared that information with the rest of the band, but we didn't mind as we were quite happy to let him get on with it. One day he would say, 'We have a recording session in London', and we never asked him how he got it or how much money was available. All the members of the band were keen to play but Dick was the only one who got down to organising things. The band might have started without him but I don't think it would have lasted all this time."

From 1954 to 1958 the Merseysippi Jazz Band recorded for the London-based jazz label, Esquire. The issues were dealt with in formal correspondence between Esquire's MD, Carlo Krahmer and the MJB's Dick Goodwin, and most of the letters from Krahmer to Goodwin have been kept. This gives a good insight into the workings of a small, independent record label in the UK in the 1950s. Esquire was a brave venture set up by an enthusiast, Carlo Krahmer - it only released jazz records and with no hit-making acts on the books, the budget was limited.

Carlo Krahmer, who was born William Max Geserick in Shoreditch in 1914, was a drummer. He had poor vision, so much so that he had been part of Claude Bampton's Orchestra, which was sponsored by the National Institute for the Blind. He worked with numerous jazz groups in the London clubs and he amassed a huge collection of jazz 78s. Just like the Wallasey Rhythm Club, he held listening sessions in his flat and he introduced many London musicians to Charlie Parker. He and his wife, Greta, established Esquire Records in 1947 and they were helped by the recording engineer, Peter Newbrook. Because the major labels were not interested, Esquire released 78s by Dizzy Gillespie and Charlie Parker in 1948. He then recorded such up-and-coming London musicians as Ronnie Scott, John Dankworth and Victor Feldman. The releases sold steadily but not sensationally and by the mid-1950s, Esquire had a substantial catalogue.

Dick Goodwin told Carlo Krahmer of the band's repertoire and the first letter on file is dated 15 October 1954. Rather clinically, Carlo told Dick that he needed "four 3 minute numbers and two 5 minute ones", the intention being to release two singles and an EP. One of the 5 minute numbers is to be "medium to slow" and the other "medium-bright". The length of the numbers was something of an obsession with Carlo who would bring a huge stopclock to the sessions and place it about an inch from his eyes. Carlo also made some suggestions from the band's repertoire and informed Dick that the recording session would be during the day on Sunday 7 November at the Voice of London studios in Marylebone Road. Carlo added, "For the six titles in question, we will pay the inclusive fee of £25." No mention of royalties and, until the final letter, no indication of sales. Perhaps a wise move: **John Lawrence (230)**: "We chose cash from Esquire as there were a lot of bands recording at the time. We felt that the market was becoming saturated and that we wouldn't sell many copies."

The session took place and two days later Carlo wrote to Dick, still formally calling him "Mr Goodwin", and made some telling remarks:

"I was very pleased with the front line but the rhythm section was not knitted together 100%. I suspect that your own bass playing was a weeny bit behind the beat which tends to make the banjo appear to be pushing the beat. However, this is merely the criticism you asked for, and maybe you can rectify this internally." The critique notwithstanding, Carlo planned to release the first sides in January 1955.

By 14 December, Mr Goodwin has become "Dick" and Esquire is issuing a 78 of 'Big Bear Stomp' and 'Daddy Do' before Christmas with an EP of the two longer tracks, 'The Mooche' and 'Sage Hen Strut' following in January. Complimentary copies were being sent and Carlo commented, "We trust you will play the discs at your club and encourage your followers to purchase same and, if you can find the time, see Hessy's in the hope that they will push local talent a little." Clearly, it was not a foregone conclusion that Merseyside shops would stock records by a local band.

Carlo gave the Merseys a Christmas present by way of a recording contract: "Esquire Records would guarantee two sessions per year similar to the previous one, at the same fee, the contract to run for two years with an option for the company to renew for a futher year." The contract itself was sent on 13 January 1955. Carlo stressed that it was "quite a usual agreement", but this does not prevent it from being restrictive. The band would be tied to Esquire and although there was an option for Esquire to extend the contract, there was no 'get out' clause for the band. This became a sticking point and Esquire amended the contract in May 1955 saying that "the agreement will automatically continue year by year until such time as either party gives notice in writing to terminate". The princely sum of £32 will be paid for each session completed and should the band record an original tune, they will receive an additional "one guinea on signature of the Copyright Indemnity".

The remaining tracks from the first session - 'Aunt Hagar's Blues' and 'Jersey Lightning' - were put on a single in February 1955. The Merseys recorded six new tracks, but with London musician Ronnie Stone depping for a sick Dick Goodwin. Two singles were released - 'Swipesy Cake Walk' / 'Whitewash Man' and 'Creole Love Call' / 'Hiawatha' - as well as an EP of two longer tracks, 'Black And Tan Fantasy' and 'Emperor Norton's Hunch'. 'The Gramophone' described 'Whitewash Man' as being 'outstandingly good' and was usually favourable to the band. Another session was set for June and Carlo added, "Don't forget to mix the tempos a little so they are not all too fast."

On 12 May 1956, Christopher Peers, who did PR for Esquire Records, told Dick Goodwin that he had sent the Radio Luxembourg DJ, David Gell, a copy of 'Blues Doctor' / 'Chicago Buzz'. He added, "To cement things from both sides, I advise you to write to Gell, giving him the usual blurb; how you listen to his programme '208 Swing Club', and how much it would help the band to get a far larger recognition. If he has not played it within the next couple of weeks, I will write to him again bucking him up, and I will ask you to do the same. In this way, we should get the disc at least one airing on Luxembourg." This resulted in a play for 'Blues Doctor' on 28 July and Chris Peers was so pleased that he asked Dick to write and thank David Gell. (In the 1970s, I met David Gell on a plane: he told me that when he reviewed records for 'Record Mirror', he would aim to have his review written before the record had finished playing.)

There was the further good news in the letter that Jack Payne had played "Swipesy Cake Walk" on the Light Programme. Encouraged by Chris, Dick dutifully wrote to Jack Payne and received a reply on 2 August 1956: "You will be pleased to hear that I received three or four very complimentary letters about your record." Did they all have Liverpool postmarks?

In January 1957, Carlo had his mind on a themed album "devoting all tunes to one or the other of the ideas previously suggested, i.e. jazz rivers, jazz rendezvous or a jazz composer. It might be a good idea to devote a session to the music of the Lu Watters band. What do you think?" The band decide upon an album of girls'names, 'All The Girls', although 'Annie Street Rock' is dedicated to a location rather than a girl. The sleeve note was to be written by Steve Voce and Carlo comments, "I hope he makes a good job of it." Following Carlo's instructions, the trumpeter Al Fairweather designed the cover, prompting these comments, "There are seven girls on the front with a title under each. For instance, 'Sweet Lorraine' has a sweet looking girl, 'When You Are I Were Young, Maggie' has a girl with the name 'Maggie' underneath, and so on throughout. In the cases of 'Mandy Lee', 'Sweet Georgia Brown' and 'Dinah Lou', we thought it very appropriate to make the girls coloured."

Dick gave Carlo an acetate by the Gin Mill Skiffle Group and their leader, Tony Davis came to see him in late April: "I had not had time to hear his record, but we went downstairs and played it over. I was not knocked out with it, and he was quite frank and thought the group was not ready for records as yet." This begs the question of why he had gone to see Carlo at all.

The interest in 'All The Girls' led Carlo to suggest a second album along the same lines and "If you do not favour the idea, how about six titles bearing on jazz haunts as previously mentioned?" Carlo requested a photograph but when he receives one of the Merseys with Louis Armstrong, he said, "This is not at all suitable for our purposes as, with Louis, it is deceiving so far are concerned for records." The titles for the next seas we ssion have been determined and again Carlo admonished the band, "Bear in mind the tempos. Not all fasts." The album became 'Mersey Tunnel Jazz' and Carlo said, "It certainly shows the band up to good advantage."

A key track on 'Mersey Tunnel Jazz' is a Humphrey Lyttelton tune, 'Hop Frog'. **John Lawrence (231)**: "Humph recorded 'Hop Frog' for Parlophone many years ago. It was a good tune so we borrowed it and recorded it. Humph wanted to re-record it a couple of years ago with his then current band and he couldn't remember how it went so he got hold of our recording."

Humphrey Lyttelton (232): "The title came from a collection of horror stories by Edgar Allen Poe, and I have a first edition. One of them is about a court jester who starts a fire and destroys the king and his guests because they maltreated a girl who was working there, Hopfrog was outraged and it sounded a nice name for a tune."

Although nothing came of it, there was talk of an album of standards by the MJB such as 'Ol' Man River', "jazzed up, as it were." The next, and final, Esquire album features rags and was called 'Any Old Rags'.

On 11 December 1958 Carlo writes to Dick Goodwin, "It is with some regret I have to inform you that the proposed session on January 18 will, I am afraid, have to be cancelled. On checking the figures of all British jazz over the past two years and in particular 1958, the sales just do not warrant further expenditure. We therefore propose not to make any British recordings during 1959, unless of course there are radical changes for the better in the sales distribution. I will contact you if and when the position improves. I would take this opportunity of wishing you and the boys the compliments of the season."

The huge sales that were about to happen in the Trad boom did not come Esquire's way. Nor the Merseys'. In December 1960 they recorded for Oriole Records, another small company but one that occasionally had big selling artists, notably Liverpool-born Russ Hamilton ("We Will Make Love", 1957) and Chas McDevitt and Nancy Whiskey ("Freight Train", also 1957). The Merseysippi Jazz Band recorded two titles for them in December 1960, Sidney Bechet's 'Funky Butt' and Scott Joplin's 'New Rag'. This was a one-off deal. There is no mention of an advance but the royalties are 3% of the retail price, which is quite reasonable for its time. They also accompanied Clinton Ford on a vo-de-o-vo EP for Oriole. **John Lawrence (233)**: "We recorded 'I Wish I Was In Peoria' with Clinton, which is an American vaudeville song. We also recorded 'Get Out And Get Under', which was written when motor cars were beginning to emerge and they were breaking down all the time." None of the Oriole recordings has been reissued, possibly because they are owned by a major company which has little interest in them.

From 1960 to 1979, the Merseysippi Jazz Band did not record at all, but since then they have recorded frequently, the LPs often being financed by themselves to sell at gigs. In the 1990s, Paul Adams, the owner of a specialist folk and jazz label, Lake Records, found the master tapes for the Esquire catalogue in a warehouse and has set about releasing them on CD. In 1997 'Mersey Tunnel Jazz' combined their 10 inch albums 'West Coast Shout' and 'Mersey Tunnel Jazz' with six other tracks.

Although the MJB made little money from their recordings, effectively the Musicians Union minimum, they did much better working for TV and radio. At first there wasn't much - their earnings from BBC for the 1956/7 tax year only amounted to £48.80, but soon they had regular work with good payments. In July 1958 they appeared on the Light Programme's 'Jazz Club' for £42.70 and travelling expenses of £6.50. This programme became 'Saturday Club' and in September 1959, March and June 1960, they received £53.80 each time. When they recorded 'The Ken Dodd Show' at the Grand Continental Theatre, Bolton in January 1960, they received £16.80 rehearsal fee and £57.75 performance fee. In April 1960 they recorded a pilot for a TV show, 'Wham!', for the producer Jack Good and each received £2.10 for rehearsals and £5.25 for performance, a total of nearly £60 for the day's work.

'The world's greatest two-trumpet band'

MM band spot

BORN on St. Valentine's Day 12 years ago, the Merseysippi Jazz Band, of Liverpool, is firmly established as one of Britain's most famous provincial semi-pro bands.

They have appeared on television and broadcast on radio; have played at London's Royal Festival Hall in a traditional jazz festival alongside Britain's top professional groups, and have cut five LPs.

A band with such drawing power and reputation would normally be expected to turn professional—but the Merseysippi have determinedly remained semi-pro.

Says bass player and manager DICK GOODWIN:

"By avoiding the nerve strain of being together all the time, as the full-time professional band must, we have avoided the break-ups and constant changing of personnel which is such a feature of the business.

"We have had the advantage of staying together as our ideas and technique developed. By turning professional we feel we would lose a great deal of the enjoyment we get from playing now."

Dick is one of the three original members of the group still with the band.

The others are KEN BALD-

WIN on banjo, and pianist FRANK ROBINSON.

Clarinettist DON LYDIAT, rated one of the best men on his instrument in the country, joined the band in 1949, and trumpeter JOHNNY LAWRENCE came in the following year.

In the autumn of 1950, the Merseysippi indulged in the most intensive three-month rehearsal in its history. Like most jazz groups, it started with a model and, after becoming immersed in its idiom, tried to evolve a style of its own. The model was the Lu Watters band.

But it was in 1952, with the arrival of another trumpeter, PETE DANIELS, that the band began to get the sound for which it became famous.

Noted for his playing and for his wit as band compère, Pete completed a two-trumpet front-line that subsequently caused many visitors to call it the greatest two-trumpet jazz band in the world.

Both trumpeters idolise Louis Armstrong — and the band always rates the highlight of its career the night it played with Satchmo at Liverpool Stadium.

TREVOR CARLISLE, on drums, and JOHN PARKES —a successor to Frank Parr, now with Mick Mulligan— were the only newcomers in the late 'fifties, though the band then began to feature singer CLINTON FORD as regular guest. He is back with them again this winter.

How long will the band last? Says Dick Goodwin: "We won't last for ever . . . but at the moment there is no sign of anyone wanting to retire."

December 24, 1960. MELODY MAKER

CHAPTER 7
TRAD MAD
Mardi Gras - Trad boom

I

Steve Voce (234): "The Merseys would stay behind after all the music had finished officially in the Cavern and we would hold jam sessions or parties there. It was Dick Goodwin's responsibility to make sure that the place was locked up and there was a big roll-down door, a massively heavy thing, that you had to reach up and pull down. This particular night we were coming out in the small hours of the morning and the two tallest guys were Ken Baldwin and John Lawrence. These two fellows with Dick in the middle were reaching up to pull it down, but Dick couldn't reach. The door came flying down and Dick, who was still trying to reach it, didn't get out of the way in time and it hit him fully on the bridge of the nose. It seemed so funny to us at the time, although it must have been excruciatingly painful. Dick clapped his hand to his nose and was running round Mathew Street in small circles shouting, 'I hate you all, I hate you all.'"

After the Cavern there could be after hours drinking at the Press Club in Lime Street, which later moved to Bold Street. **Ken Baldwin (235)**: "The Press Club was for members of the press but they accepted associate members. Alan Sytner was an associate member. Dick Goodwin joined and then I joined, and this was a marvellous place. It was a way of drinking late, and Cecil the barman would stay there as long as you did. Everytime you bought a round, you'd say, 'Will you have one, Cecil?' and he would say, 'Aye'. 'How much is it, Cecil?' 'Eight and sixpence for yours and with mine, nine and six.' Cecil had his own crate round the back and he would put bottles of Blue Label into it. He would drink them in his own time. When the London bands came up to play, we would take the drinking members - they didn't all drink - to the Press Club and we might drink there all night. No ladies were allowed but there were card games. We would get jolly and hilarious and dawn would break at six o'clock. People would say, 'It can't be very late, the buses are still running', but we'd been there all night. Usually we would break up around two or three and Dick's mother would get extremely annoyed at times. One night he

111

couldn't get in 'cause he couldn't find his key so he sat in the porch and nodded off. In the morning his mother found Dick in the porch and she said, 'Dick, what are on earth are you doing?' and he said, 'I'm waiting to pay the milkman.'"

By 1956 Frank Parr had moved to London to play in Mick Mulligan's band. **John Lawrence (236)**: "The Mick Mulligan Band was without any doubt a one-off. They were professionals and so they spent all their time touring the country. We as a semi-pro band would only go outside Liverpool once a week. We weren't a touring band and we didn't get involved in the life that they had. They had a lot of parties and drinking and general fun, but even among professional bands, the Mick Mulligan Band was a one-off. We were a very watered-down version of that."

George Melly wrote about his exploits in one of the funniest books about life on the road, 'Owning-Up' **Chris Barber (237)**: "'Owning-Up' was an accurate picture of what it was like for George Melly but it wasn't the same for all of us because we're not all like George Melly, I could say thank goodness. He's a ribald and libertarian character and he lived that life to the full. Once you're known as that sort of character, those sort of things begin happening to you as you appeal to other people who are like that."

Ever tactful, I asked **George Melly (238)** if his lifestyle ever affected his performance? "You mean, was I ever too drunk to perform? Yes, frequently, and not only then. We thought it was a tremendous lark and we were always getting drunk. I was frequently forgetting my words and mumbling and falling about, as indeed were the rest of the band as we went through that transitional period from being semi-pro to pro. Once we hit the road and were faced the reality of earning a living, we thought we'd better pull our socks up and present the audiences with what they had paid to hear."

Frank Parr (239): "The Mardi Gras was a very good jazz club on Mount Pleasant, very civilised by the standards of the time, and we would all retire to the Press Club for a drink after hours and it could stay open all night. On one of my more bizarre escapades, we had a few drinks in the Press Club and I was going to be staying with my parents, who were living in Wallasey. As I passed out at the

Press Club, the driver Pete Appleby threw me over his shoulder in a fireman's lift and threw me in the back of the wagon. The next thing I knew I woke up at Finchley Road underground station. Then I had to make my way to Euston, get the train back to Liverpool and turn up at my mum's the next afternoon saying, 'Sorry, Mum, we went to a party last night.'"

II

The Merseysippi Jazz Band undertook all manner of bookings. **Frank Robinson (240)**: "We did something for the 750th anniversary of Liverpool's charter and we went on a lorry around the tenements in the south end of Liverpool and Sefton Park. The lorry would stop in the street and we would play, but the piano was rubbish. The festival lasted about a week and if there was no one around, we would end up in the pub."

John Lawrence (241): "One of the venues was off Princes Avenue and there was nobody about. We went into a drinking club in Hemans Street for a quick drink, but we stayed there for the whole of the time we should have been playing."

In January 1958 the Merseysippi Jazz Band played at the Royal Albert Hall - at four in the morning. **John Lawrence (242)**: "It was one of those multi-band concerts where each band would try and upstage the others. You always started with the loudest and fastest tune you could manage. In complete contrast, the Graeme Bell Band started with a very slow Duke Ellington tune and brought the house down as nobody else had thought of doing that. We had been waiting to play since 10 pm because an all-night session was quite a novelty, there was a huge crowd there. We had Clint with us and there was a song at the top of the charts, 'Ma, He's Making Eyes At Me' by the Johnny Otis Show, which had a Bill Haley flavour about it. Clint thought it was a good tune and that we should try it. It was an easy tune and we played it well but a song that was at the top of the hit parade was anathema to the serious jazz fans, even if it was an oldie. The stage at the Albert Hall is pretty high so, as with the Proms, the stage is chin high to the people who are standing. One die-hard shouted out, 'You're not fit to lick Ken Colyer's boots.' We thought this was hilarious so his whole outburst misfired completely. Why people should get so worked up over what they think is authentic music, I don't know."

Pete Daniels, who looked a hybrid of Michael Bentine and Harry Secombe, was known for his witty stage announcements. He was also a member of the Liverpool SF Group and in 1958 he arranged an appearance by the Merseys at a science fiction convention in London. **Bill Harry (243)**: "Everyone in the Liverpool society had a good sense of humour and we used to meet and drink at a pub in Bold Street. Ian and Norma Sharrock ran the club and Ian was a philatelist with a shop in Dale Street. Broadly speaking, there were two types of science fiction: the British writers had the world being destroyed by plagues and droughts while the American writers were more interested in huge, big galactic wars. There was a convention in London in 1958 and I remember going there with Michael Moorcock."

III

The Cavern was going so well that it had a membership of 25,000 by 1959. The First Springtime Jazz Festival, which included Humphrey Lyttelton, was a great success. Professional musicians working at the Grafton or Reece's would come to the Cavern to jam when they had finished. Alan Sytner had introduced lunchtime sessions (a brilliant innovation) and bingo afternoons to bring in more revenue. The club was thriving and both of Alan's parents helped with the administration. The Cavern also mounted successful events on board the Royal Iris and the Royal Daffodil, thus emulating the riverboats in New Orleans. The boats would take audiences up and down the Mersey - a genuine case of the music going round and round.

But two things pushed the Cavern off course. One was Alan Sytner's lavish playboy lifestyle and the other was that beat music was threatening jazz's popularity, and Alan had no interest in that. **Alan Sytner (244)**: "Whatever they played, it was all crap. Not just the Beatles, all of them, but it was very popular and people wanted it to happen. Wednesday night was talent night, but I didn't want to turn the club into no talent nights."

By June 1959 it looked as though the Cavern might have to close in view of Alan Sytner's debts. **John Parkes (245)**: "I can remember

Alan Sytner putting the Cavern up for sale. He wanted £2,000 and he said that anyone who had £2,000 could have it. After one lunchtime jazz session, I went to see my nan, my mother's mother, to see if she'd lend me £2,000. She had £2,000 but she wouldn't let me have it because it sounded too precarious."

Ray McFall (246), who worked for Sytner's accountants, bought the lease: "I took the Cavern over as a jazz club in the later stages of Alan Sytner's ownership. The club's fortunes were going down and it was obvious that there was a tremendous interest for beat music. Skiffle had come and gone and I felt that I had to introduce beat music steadily, which worked very well. It took two or three years for jazz to be phased out but some bands like Acker Bilk's retained their popularity. He opened the club for me and maintained regular appearances throughout."

Ray McFall booked the Swinging Blue Jeans for a weekly guest night, a skilful move as they had a foot in both camps. **Ralph Ellis (247)**: "We had a jazz flavour but we had a front lineup of three guitars rather than sax, trombone and trumpet. We had a trad jazz feel but with a Merseybeat sound about it. In the end the people wanted rock'n'roll. Bob Wooler has never got over the fact that we changed to rock'n'roll as he thought we had a unique sound, but we wanted to make records that would sell."

Ken Baldwin (248): "I wasn't really aware of local beat music until they started these shows at the New Brighton Tower and they must have put on half a dozen groups at a time. I can't really criticise the groups because they were pinching American songs just like us, but at the time we never bothered listening to them. It was electric noise and we were very much against that. We were so anti-beat music that we never stopped to speak to them and ask them how they were doing."

Don Lydiatt (249): "Amplifiers had just come in and you could pick up a guitar and get a great sound. However, you couldn't pick up a trombone or clarinet or trumpet and get a great sound - it takes hours of learning. It's remarkable when you think about it. These people had no real desire to play their instruments or undertake any proper learning, but they could get a good sound. Some of the groups were good - the Swinging Blue Jeans used to be at the

Mardi and they were very good."

How much does the MJB remember about the Beatles? **Don Lydiatt (250)**: "Very little - about as much as they remember about us, I should think. The pseudo-skiffle cum beat groups came on in the interval and we beat it out to the Beaconsfield. John Lennon referred to us as 'Those old bastards' and they were just another young group coming up."

John Lawrence (251): "I remember with some embarrassment that when we came off stage to go to the pub and they came on stage, we never spoke to each other. We had a barely-concealed contempt for each other. We were older than they were and later on John Lennon described us as the old buggers who didn't want them on stage, which was correct. We lived in different worlds."

Hil Hughes (252): "I sang with the Climax Jazz Band at the Cavern and when I'd finished, John Lennon said to me, 'You're singing like Ella Fitzgerald and Bessie Smith. Why don't you sing like yourself?' I thought he was attacking me but he was really giving me the biggest compliment of my life as he thought I sounded like them."

Alf Tweedle (253): "We played at the Iron Door after the Beatles had done a tour of Germany and we were playing dance band and Dixieland stuff. There was a poster that said, 'Welcome to the fabulous Beatles' and I said to the clarinet player, 'Have you ever heard such a stupid name?'. I have a poster from 1962 of the Tower Ballroom, New Brighton and we played a job there as Alf Tweedle's Dixielanders and it was 7/6d (37p) and 5s (25p) to see the Beatles."

Mike McCombe (254), then with Noel Walker's Stompers: "We did a gig at the Iron Door with the Beatles who had become the band to listen to. They had made a name for themselves and John Lennon told the audience not to be disruptive and to listen to the band."

Don Lydiatt (255): "The change happened very quickly. One January we were booked to top the bill at a festival at Bury Golf Club in July. Come July the whole thing had overturned, the audience only wanted to see the beat groups and we were met by hordes of screaming kids. Later on, we found out that the groups were as astounded as we were. They hardly had to sing as the fans screamed solidly and they certainly didn't want us on stage."

Kenny Ball (256): "I remember the Beatles doing the interval for us at the Cavern and I had never seen guys in all-leather suits before. It can't have been much fun for them as it was very damp down there. The fellers liked us and the girls liked them and I thought there must be something wrong with us."

Chris Barber (257): "We never played the Cavern but we did concerts every six months in Liverpool, usually at the Phil. We did meet the Beatles a couple of times and bought them drinks and were friendly. The Beatles were quite surprised because I don't think they'd met any jazz musicians who'd been friendly before. It didn't stop John making his famous pronouncement that he didn't like jazz."

George Melly (258): "We used to play the Bodega in Manchester on Saturday and the Cavern on Sunday. It was before the Beatles were well known, but gradually the Liverpool sound became popular, in Liverpool first of all, and the Beatles used to play in our interval. We ran over to the Grapes and Lennon always resented British jazz very much. He used to say that these old men had got in his way and he would have been more successful earlier. My father much preferred it when we moved from the Cavern to Mardi Gras as it was a much more commodious place."

Although the Beatles found success at the Cavern in Ray McFall's tenure, **Alan Sytner (259)** is sure of his place in history: "Without me no Cavern, without me no Beatles, without me none of the bloody things really. If there had not been a Cavern, none of this would have happened. The talent came out at the Cavern, there was nowhere else and there wouldn't have been anywhere else because the Cavern created a precedent. People opened the Mardi Gras and the Iron Door and all the others, but they didn't think of it for themselves: they looked at the Cavern and created an alternative. None of the owners had any interest in music or knew anything about music. They thought it was a good business and jumped on the bandwagon. I don't think any of this would have happened without me. Obviously, Lennon and McCartney were geniuses, but would they have flourished without the Cavern? If they had been playing in church halls in Maghull, would anyone have taken any notice?"

IV

In the wake of Alan Sytner's initial success, many new clubs had opened on Merseyside. Jimmy Ireland had tried jazz at the Minorca Coffee Bar in Tarleton Street and then he opened the Mardi Gras, which had been the Crompton Club, on 30 October 1958. It was in Mount Pleasant and near the Adelphi Hotel. The advertisements stressed that the club was very different from the Cavern: "Come and enjoy genuine jazz in luxurious surroundings." It had carpets and furniture, was licensed and could admit the same numbers as the Cavern. The Mardi had top-line guests including John Dankworth, Kenny Ball and, most significantly, Muddy Waters. **Brian Linford (260)**, who managed the Mardi Gras: "Kenny Ball was on the first week that the Mardi opened. Unfortunately, he felt that his loyalty was to the Iron Door. There was a difference between the Mardi Gras and the Cavern as they had their jazz bands and we had ours. When the Cavern decided to abandon jazz,we took on most of the jazz bands that were playing in the Cavern."

The Merseysippi Jazz Band terminated their residency at the Cavern in May 1959 and moved to the Mardi. **John Parkes (261)**: "The Mardi Gras was packed every night and I don't remember a bad night at the Mardi. I thoroughly enjoyed it and I liked all the guest bands like Acker Bilk's and Kenny Ball's."

Ralph Watmough (262): "The Mardi Gras was far superior to the Cavern. It was a much superior set-up as it was a genuine night club and we used to have some very good sessions there."

Valerie Dicks (263): "There was rivalry between the Cavern and the Mardi Gras, but the Cavern was definitely the place to see someone. It had atmosphere whereas the Mardi was up-market and didn't quite make it. I associate jazz with dark, dank, seedy places."

John Chilton (264): "I often came to Liverpool to play and it was always marvellous if the Merseys were on the same bill with us at the Mardi. I knew it was going to be a good evening and I could stand at the bar during my time off and hear some damn good jazz. Jim Ireland was my great pal and there was a period when he often had a jazz group on with a skiffle or a beat group. The beat groups played opposite jazz attractions at the Mardi and you could sense that something was going to change. Soon the beat groups were the main attraction."

Kenny Ball (265): "A piano player called Cecil came up to me one night after we'd done a show at the Mardi Gras and said, 'You should record this - it's a lovely song called 'Samantha' from 'High Society'.' It was a lovely song and we rehearsed it and actually played a much longer version than the record. The chord sequence is so lovely. It's different to any other chord sequence in the key of C and the first chord is a B 7th, a semitone below the major, which is an intriguing start to any tune."

'I Love You Samantha' became Kenny Ball's first hit record so perhaps it's a pity that Cecil didn't make this suggestion to the Merseys. **Ken Baldwin (266)** explains: "We had Clinton with us at the Mardi and Kenny Ball realised his potential and offered him a job. He would only sing four or five numbers with Kenny as Kenny was singing a lot of the songs himself. Clint found that he was waiting at the side so he went off as a solo act and did very well."

Clinton Ford (267): "I was at the Mardi Gras and Kenny Ball had seen me. I got a phone call asking me to join his band. I thought twice about it as I didn't want to leave Liverpool, but Jimmy Ireland at the Mardi Gras talked me into it. He said, 'You'll never really make anything here but down there you'll have an international audience.' I joined them and Kenny wanted me to play banjo as well, which I could do, but I didn't want to take the banjo player's job, who was a lovely chap. Kenny couldn't afford to keep me after awhile and so I went on my own. We were doing 'Easy Beat' on Sunday mornings and when I told Brian Mathew that I had been given the push and wouldn't be on ' Easy Beat' anymore, he said, 'Oh yes you will because we will give you your own contract.'"

Clinton had joined Kenny Ball and his Jazzmen in 1960 and was only with them for a few months. As a solo act, he received plenty of TV work via 'Stars And Garters', 'The Good Old Days' and 'The Billy Cotton Band Show'. He had his own series, 'Clinton's Cakewalk', on the Light Programme. When Derek Taylor interviewed him for 'Melody Maker' in 1963, he kept repeating that he was tired. Yet despite the occasional chart success, Clinton Ford never made it to the top. **Clinton Ford (268)**: "I can't be put in a pigeonhole and when people ask me what sort of songs I sing, I say, 'The ones with words and music.' Even 'Old Shep' seemed like a good idea at the time. Red Foley had written it and Hank Snow had recorded a definitive version. Elvis Presley made a lousy version and I'm sure the Jordanaires are out of tune. I had done it on stage and seen the reaction and I said to the Levys who owned Oriole that I wanted to do it but they didn't like it. I talked them into letting me record it but they wouldn't release it. It came time for my contract to terminate. I said, 'If you don't release 'Old Shep', I'm going, I know it's going to be a hit.' I went in to terminate the contract and Reg Warburton, the recording manager, said, 'Before you go any further, 'Old Shep' is being released next week.' I said, 'Okay I'm staying', and it was a hit."

John Parkes (269): "Clinton has always been a good-hearted bloke and he said he would give his royalties on 'Old Shep' to the dogs' home. As it happened, it hit the jackpot and the money all went to the dogs' home, so poor Clint missed out yet again."

Ironically, at the same time as beat groups were taking over the Cavern and the Mardi, trad jazz was making the UK charts. It started with Monty Sunshine playing 'Petite Fleur' as part of Chris Barber's Jazz Band in 1959 and was followed in 1960 by the similar 'Summer Set' from Acker Bilk and his Paramount Jazz Band. Kenny Ball hit home with 'I Love You Samantha' and for a couple of years, both Ball and Bilk had several hits. 'It's Trad, Dad!', directed by Richard Lester in 1962, may have a silly story but it is a wonderful documentary of jazz bands of the period.

Monty Sunshine left Chris Barber's Jazz Band in 1960. **John Lawrence (270)**: "I gave going professional a lot of thought as Monty Sunshine invited me to join his band. I agonised over that for quite a long time, but I felt that giving up a reasonably successful job to take a chance was too much of a risk, and I didn't think I was up to it anyway. I'm very glad that I didn't accept the offer, and probably so is Monty. Really, I think that to be a professional musician, like a professional cricketer or golfer, you have got to be pretty damn good, and there are a lot of people who are good but not pretty damn good. You've got to be realistic and say, 'I know how good I am and that isn't good enough.' You have a certain built-in talent and once you have made use of that talent, you're not going to get any better. I had reached a plateau and I knew that was as good as I was going to get."

Don Lydiatt (271): "We maintained our independence in as much as we refused to do hit parade tunes. We didn't do 'Petite Fleur' or 'Stranger On The Shore'. We used to say, 'If we made a record and it was a hit, would we turn pro?', but we didn't think it would happen."

John Lawrence (272): "We were asked to turn professional but we were too busy doing other things. We were all employed and we didn't want to risk giving up the day job by turning professional. At the time there were a lot of bands doing well and selling records, but we were wise enough to realise that it wasn't going to last. If we had done that, we would have fallen by the wayside after a few years. The 3Bs of Ball, Barber and Bilk are still successful but there is only room for three or four major bands today."

Pat Halcox (273) plays trumpet with Chris Barber's Jazz Band: "I enjoyed the boom as we got good crowds. I wasn't married at the time so it was nice in other ways too. However, the music, instead of getting better, was getting worse. There were a lot of very bad bands. Clubs opened everywhere and they all needed live sounds. The trad era killed itself by having to employ so many bad musicians."

Humphrey Lyttelton (274): "A lot of musicians had no knowledge of , or affection for, the New Orleans style and trad became a vehicle for funny uniforms and glorified pub singalongs, and a lot of people had the idea that this was what jazz was all about. It became very, very popular in the dance halls but when the next generation came along, the music was discarded - there was a backlash against jazz simply because it was last year's music."

George Melly (275): "Trad came in at the end of the 50s, but it got to be a very monotonous sound and the bands were swept away by the Beatles and the Rolling Stones. Jazz was a very dirty word from '63 to '68. I was in a band that wasn't particularly traddy and didn't have that amplified banjo noise, but I got out of jazz just before the Beatles broke. I wanted to stay in London and I started to have some success as a journalist. Luckily, I jumped off the bandwagon just before it fell over the cliff."

Clinton Ford and Dan Lydiatt at the Royal Albert Hall, 1958

" S A T U R D A Y   C L U B "   (10)

The best of today's 'Pop' entertainment

featuring

EDDIE COCHRAN

GENE VINCENT AND THE WILDCATS

AL SAXON

MIKE PRESTON

THE ZODIACS

THE BERT WEEDON QUARTET

THE GEOFF TAYLOR QUINTET

****

"Cat's Call"

Disc stars you've requested

****

'The Jazz Cellar'

THE MERSEYSIPPI JAZZ BAND
with
CLINTON FORD

****

"New To You"

Spinning the latest releases

****

Introduced by Brian Matthew

PRODUCED BY:

JIMMY GRANT
****

TRANSMISSION: SATURDAY, MARCH 12th 1960: 10.00a.m. - 12.00noon
                                          LIGHT PROGRAMME:

REHEARSAL: 8.15 a.m. 3A. B.H.   TLO: 9802

S.M.   Ron Belchier: A.S.M. Charles Clark-Maxwell
XP. Op: Bernard Andrews:

MERSEYSIPPI JAZZ BAND: Reh: 9.00 a.m. PLAYHOUSE, MANCHESTER

REH: with TALK-BACK: 9.15 - 10.00 a.m.

****

Saturday Club Programme

CHAPTER 8
BACK O' TOWN BLUES
Liverpool residencies - Jill Martin

I

By 1963 the city was awash with beat music. **Ken Baldwin (276)**: "For a short time, jazz was the popular music of the day. The jazz bands became more commercial because they were professionals and the audiences were their bread and butter. Then it declined. The years from 1963 to 1973 were bleak years for jazz."

The Merseysippi Jazz Band had fewer engagements, but they had their moments. **Brian Linford (277)**: "Jimmy Ireland was always looking for ways to make the Mardi bigger. It was always so popular and so busy, but the acoustics were terrible. It had originally been a cinema and the ceiling was 40 feet high, and the only way to increase the capacity was by going up. We decided to build a balcony and it was completed by Christmas 1963, but because we had overloaded the system, all the lights fused. The main fuse was located in Turner's auction room down below. We didn't want to stand on ceremony looking for the key holder, so we broke in. We had the fuse repaired, but we got a solicitor's letter from Mr Duffy, the owner of the auction room. After that, we moved the fuses into the Mardi Gras and installed a new system. We were lucky when it happened that the Merseys were playing. They were acoustic and could play in the dark."

The MJB played at the Mardi Gras until 1964. **Don Lydiatt (278)**: "We left the Mardi and we moved to a pub in Edmund Street, two things happen when you get older - first of all, your memory goes and I can't remember the second - oh, it was the Cross Keys and we played to 30 people, just to keep together really."

Tony Brown (279): "The trad boom only lasted a couple of years but the music resettled. Suddenly there was no need to pander to what these people wanted to hear. The audiences went to listen to good music and the bands started playing proper jazz again."

And have a drink. **Ken Baldwin (280)**: "Dick Goodwin fell off the stage once. We used to take the stage somewhat inebriated at times and Dick was standing at the back. One minute Dick was there and the next minute he wasn't. He had taken a step backwards and gone through the curtains. He didn't hurt himself but he did drop about three feet."

A typical Dick Goodwin story concerns a gig at a swimming baths. **Don Lydiatt (281):** "You had to walk through a little foot-bath before you were allowed in the water and Dick went, 'Come on fellows we're on'. He turned and stomped through the foot-bath in his shoes and socks and he squelched to the stand and had to play with wet feet. The rest of us all walked round it. Another time in the Masonic off Dale Street, he was trying to get through the door with his bass and it moved the bridge. He screamed at the janitor, 'Inadequate door facilities'. That became a phrase in the band for some years."

Dick Goodwin had woodworm in his bass and he took it in at Hessy's. They tightened the strings and the whole thing turned to powder. **Tony Barrow (282):** "Dick Goodwin was the band's manager and booker. I booked them for one of my Jazz Band Balls at St Luke's Hall in Crosby for £20. A rider in the contract called for a bottle of Scotch in the band room, which had to be smuggled in as we were on church premises. The Scotch was for Dick's personal consumption."

John Lawrence (283): "Dick Goodwin knew that he wasn't the best bass player in the world and he felt that he had gone as far as he could. He heard Derek Vaux and realised he was a much better bass player and would make the band sound better, so Derek joined us in 1964. Dick also had the sheer physical problem of getting to and from gigs with his double-bass because he didn't have a car, so he decided to stop playing and just manage the band."

John Higham (284): "Dick knew the exact fare for driving him home and he would regularly argue with the drivers and his conversation always ended with, 'I'll see you in Hudd Street in the morning'."

Ken Baldwin (285): "Dick knew that he wasn't a great musician and that the music was overtaking him. He preferred to drop a few gins and look after the welfare of the band and that's what he did. He came with us on the gigs and he would oversee things and receive the money at the end of the night."

Dick Goodwin played a left-handed bass so he couldn't pick up anyone else's. After he left, he had once had too much to drink at Blackpool's North Pier and he went on stage and started playing Derek Vaux's bass. Pete Daniels looked around to see what had happened and he was chased off stage. **John Lawrence (286)**: "Dick still came to all the gigs but I don't think he ever played again. The companionship was the main element as far as he was concerned. He had the enthusiasm and the ability to make sure that a group of seven or eight fellows would turn up somewhere to play for a sensible fee. Even when he asked John Parkes to take over the administration, he still came along almost every week."

II

The Merseysippi Jazz Band did not record from 1961 to 1979 so there is no permanent record of their work with Jill Martin. Without any reservations, everyone in the Merseys thought she was an excellent vocalist and, in John Lawrence's words, she was "the sort of singer every band dreams of". Two private recordings of Jill with the MJB in 1965 were included on their 1999 CD, 'Senior Moments' - 'I Can't Believe That You're In Love With Me' and 'Melancholy Blues'. **Ken Baldwin (287)**: "We heard Gladys Martin singing in a country and western group at the Cavern in 1958. We thought that she had a lovely voice and we asked her to join us. We renamed her Jill Martin as the name 'Gladys' did not look right on a poster." (Where the MJB first heard Jill Martin sing is a point of contention. The other possibility is when she was singing with a beat group on the Royal Iris.)

Phil Taylor (288): "I had a company car and I used to travel to London with them, and Jill Martin would always be in my car. They did a gig one Friday night and on the Saturday they were at a BBC broadcast of 'Saturday Club'. It was Jill's mum's birthday and the compere Brian Matthew asked Jill if she wanted to say happy birthday. Jill said very quickly, 'Mrs Martin, 17 Tupman Street, Dingle, Liverpool 8: hello, mum, happy birthday'. She did it in two seconds flat, and it brought the house down. It was a very memorable moment."

Jill Martin enjoyed having fun with lyrics. The title line of 'Nobody Knows You When You're Down And Out' became 'Nobody knows you when it's hanging out'. "I saw a man who danced with his wife" in 'Chicago' was changed to "I saw a man on top of his wife". 'It's The Talk Of The Town' became a homage to a large erection, 'It's The Stalk Of The Town'. **Phil Taylor (289)**: "Jill only had one lung but she had the most powerful voice I've ever heard singing jazz. When I play the tape with 'Melancholy Blues' on, I can feel the tears coming on. One time we were all staying in a 30 bob a night hotel in London. Around the dining room were busts of famous people and she said, 'Bloody hell, what a name, In I Go Jones.' She had no idea who Inigo Jones was. . She was such a lovely person. Her real name was Gladys and we all called her Glad, and her favourite expression was 'Up your bum'."

Mike McCombe (290): "I knew of Jill because the Merseys were always talking about her, but I hadn't seen her. I had a job driving a truck and I was spending an evening in Gateshead. I was walking around, looking for somewhere to have a drink and I heard this singing coming from a working man's club. It was obviously a Liverpool girl and at the end of set, I introduced myself. I told her that I played with the Merseys and she said, 'I used to sing with them' and it was Jill Martin. Eventually she got tired of travelling and she settled back in Liverpool. She would come and sing with us at that Greenall's pub by the Royal Court, the Sportsman. She was a lovely person with a lovely personality and a great voice."

Jill Martin suffered poor health and died in 1977. **John Parkes (291)**: "I was the manager of the band then and was living in Spain part of the time in a house I'd bought from George Chisholm. Mike McCombe sent me a telegram saying that Jill had died so you can imagine the shock. I knew she'd been ill but I'd never thought about her dying. She'd died of a brain haemorrhage so I came home the next day to help at Jill's funeral. At the time I was arranging a trip to Toronto for the band and on the day of the funeral, we heard that we weren't going after all. It was bad news all round as we were all geared up for going. The wives were going with us, they'd bought special clothes, and it all fell through. That was the worst day in the Merseys' history."

After Jill Martin's death, the MJB acquired another vocalist, Jan Sutherland. **Mike McCombe (292)**: "Jan Sutherland used to play with the Blue Mags before they were the Blue Mags. I used to play with the Blue Mags and she turned up one night. As soon as I heard her, I thought, ' This is the girl who could replace Jill', so she sat in with the band a couple of times and eventually came on board. She was much more of a red hot mama than Jill was. Jill was a real good singer but Jan was more of a belter."

John Lawrence (293): "Jan Sutherland was a solo singer around the clubs and ironically, we met her for the first time at Jill's funeral. We were at a low ebb as we had just lost a great singer with great potential of whom we were very fond. Jan knew a lot of our songs and she liked jazz - in particular, Bessie Smith. She was keen on singing jazz and wanted to sing with a band. We were very pleased to give it a go and it worked very well."

Ken Baldwin (294): "Jan was a pro who would do the night clubs and she was extremely good, an act on her own. She had a baby at home in Southport and as she didn't want to go touring anymore, playing with us was ideal. She was with us for about four years. I don't mind vocalists, but they do have a terrible habit of taking over the band. They love singing and if you let them, you would play two numbers to start the evening, two numbers before the interval and two to start the second set and they would sing all the rest. These days we don't have a vocalist but most of us have a little go. Don, Pete and myself all sing."

In 1968 Clinton Ford had his greatest moment - an hilarious album with George Chisholm and the Inmates called 'Clinton The Clown'. **Clinton Ford (295)**: "I mixed it up too much. I was recording sentimental songs one day and comedy the next. People didn't know what I was going to do next and my record sales suffered as a consequence. The 'Clinton The Clown' album with George Chisholm was great fun to record. We did it in an all night session and I fell asleep against the wall at four o'clock in the morning waiting for the taxi to go home. Johnny Stevens wrote 'My Baby's Wild About My Old Trombone' for George and myself. It's very hard on the lip for a trombonist to clown around like that, but Pete Fryer is as funny as Chisholm when we do it."

John Lawrence (296): "A lot of the music we do is just fun - we don't take ourselves or our music too seriously. 'My Baby's Wild About My Old Trombone' involves some very comic trombone playing and Pete Fryer can't wait to make a fool of himself when we do it. The audience wants an enjoyable evening and it is a different world from the way it started. The audience today does not consist of jazz experts and sometimes one of us will do a solo that is not all that interesting and still get a round of applause."

I was intrigued to see Clinton Ford and Phil Taylor listed as the writers of 'The Old Fashioned Bustle My Grandmother Wore', but it's not strictly correct. **Phil Taylor (297)**: "My parents were in ENSA during the war and before that my father ran a concert party in Liverpool. They had a comedian, Billy Rowlands, in ENSA who sang 'The Old Fashioned Bustle My Grandmother Wore' to the tune of 'The Mountains Of Mourne' and he had written the words himself. He had never copyrighted them and he had no family when he died in 1945 at the age of 90. I wrote the words down for Clint and he wrote a new tune for it and recorded it with George Chisholm. I happened to be working in London that week and Clint invited me to the session and I watched it being sung at two o'clock in the morning."

Looking through the Merseysippi Jazz Band's personnel in Appendix 1, you will notice that the drummer has the hot seat and some incumbents only last a few weeks. Without question, the most famous member of the Merseysippi Jazz Band has been Aynsley Dunbar. Now he is one of the world's most respected drummers, but as a teenager in the 1960s, he had a stint with the Merseys. Not for want of trying, I have been unable to interview Aynsley Dunbar for this book. However, in a career retrospective, he did mention his days with the Merseysippi Jazz Band to the journalist, Rick Mattingly: "All the other guys were about forty and were married. They all worked in the daytime and they'd come together at night to play jazz. During one of my first gigs with them, they gave me a drum solo. So I'm up there playing away and I decided it was time I finished, and all of a sudden I looked over at the bar, and they're all sitting by the bar drinking, so my drum solo lasted about 20 minutes. Nowadays I get complaints about long drum solos, but they wanted me to keep going so they could go to the bar and have a drink."

Don Lydiatt (298): "Aynsley Dunbar was interested in rock more than jazz and he didn't stay all that long. He wasn't a bad drummer. Someone told me that he had gone to America and done all sorts of things, but I didn't follow his career." When I told Don that it wasn't just anyone but Frank Zappa, he said, "Was it really? Well, he must have improved."

After a succession of short order drummers, **Mike McCombe (299)** joined them in 1967: "I was with Ken Colyer for six months but I had my family in Liverpool. I had to live somewhere in London and I couldn't afford two places. I came back here on a Friday night and Derek Vaux rang me as soon as I was back and I joined in with the band on Sunday night. I wasn't really doing what they wanted as I was playing press rolls, which is a New Orleans style, whereas they were more West Coast and the style was more like Eddie Condon's drummer. I soon adapted and I stayed until 1982 when I left for family reasons, nothing to do with them as I loved playing with them."

Mike McCombe now lives in San Francisco and he plays on cruise liners with the Grand Dominion Jazz Band. **Mike McCombe (300)**: "I hate drum solos and I won't take them. I don't mind doing a four bar breakdown now and again or eight bars at the end of a tune, but I won't take the LBDS, the long boring drum solo."

III

In the 1970s the MJB struggled to find an audience. **Derek Vaux (301)**: "The worst gigs were at the Sportsman's Bar on Wednesday nights: it was next to the Royal Court theatre and it was a swine to get parked and unloaded, especially when you're carrying a double-bass. They were barren years as jazz wasn't popular. The pub would be full at seven o'clock and as soon as we started to play, the place would empty instantly - and I do mean 'instantly'. It was desperately depressing to see people drinking up and fleeing as quickly as they could. The place would then slowly fill up with jazz fans for the rest of the evening. The band kept together and retained its sense of humour but looking back, it was awful."

Tony Brown (302) recalls a similar experience with another band: "The worst gig I can recall was in East London many years ago with a few youngsters who were pop fans and eventually cleared off. At the end we went to quarrel with the guv'nor telling him that he shouldn't have booked us here. 'Hang on', he said, 'I was only paying you to clear the place, I want to have family nights here. The brewery is doing the place up and I want to get rid of the kids.'"

John Lawrence (303): "When you're semi-pro, you can't pick and choose your venues. If somebody offers Chris Barber an engagement in a place he doesn't like the look of, he can say, 'No thanks.' When you're semi-pro, you grab all you can and you play some hell-holes. Not only are they smoky and damp like the Cavern in the early years, but sometimes it's a bad venue and the audience aren't the slightest bit interested in what you're doing. You've got to take the rough with the smooth and very often it's more rough than smooth. The funny thing is that if you play ten gigs and nine of them are not a lot of fun, the tenth one where the venue is right, the sound is right and the audience is enthusiastic can make it all worthwhile. One good gig is worth nine bad ones. Any jazz musician will tell you that."

Don Lydiatt (304): "We started to do some jobs at Swansea University and that led to one in Neath, which is just outside Swansea. It was a Wednesday night in the middle of winter, and Wednesday afternoon was my half-day. We hired a coach to take us down and it came with a driver and a navigator. We got there and did the gig. We had a meal and set off about one in the morning. We started off and we found out that we were heading for The Wash, and off we went again. At 6 in the morning, it was snowing and there was a signpost pointing in the direction we were going and saying 'Neath - 16 miles'. We were hysterical with laughter but we laughed at anything then. I had to open the shop and as my wife was staying with her mother, I had to ring Frank's wife. It had become a snowstorm and we stopped at the next phone box. It was steamed up with somebody inside. Eventually she opened the door and said, 'Do you want to use the phone?'. I said, 'Yes' and she said, 'Go in, I'm only waiting for a bus.' We arrived home in time to open the shop after dinner at two o'clock and I'd had no sleep at all."

John Lawrence (305): "Let me tell you about the busiest week of my life. It wasn't with the Merseys at all. The Acker Bilk Band was coming to Liverpool and they were booked for two shows a night, one at the Shakespeare and the other at Allinsons at Litherland. Their trumpet player Al Fairweather couldn't make it and they asked me to play with Acker. I said, 'When?' and they said, 'Next week. Every night, twice.' I had a business to run but they said, 'Please help us out.' In reality, I jumped at the chance as it was like a Royal Command Performance. Everyday I would finish work at the office, put on a clean shirt and play two concerts with the Bilk band who were into fairly serious carousing. I would get back in the middle of the night, get three hours' sleep and then get up and do the whole thing again. I don't know how I survived but it was tremendous fun."

Dennis Gracey (306): "In a sense, I'm glad I left the Merseys as I don't think I could have coped with playing and a full-time job. I did a gig with the Blue Mags a few years ago and it involved leaving Rainhill at 2pm on a Friday and playing from eight until midnight somewhere south of Bristol. We drove back and when I got home at four in the morning, I thought, 'Well, this isn't for me.'"

Don Lydiatt (307): "We'd been playing in Sheffield. Coming back, we were full of ale and it was misty. We stopped on top of the Snake Pass for a pee and there was a grass verge, grass moorland and a low wall which we climbed over and stood on the other side to relieve ourselves, but Clinton took an extra step forwards and we heard this howl. We couldn't see a thing so we got some newspapers and lit them and dropped them down and we could see Clinton on a ledge. He had fallen 20 feet, but it was sloping so he had rolled down. Below him, it was a 100 foot drop into the canyon at the bottom. He started crawling up and we were leaning over to get him. He calls it the night the Merseys saved his life."

And yes, the Merseys had their own Bob the Builder to sing novelty songs. **Bob Ross (308)**: "I was with the Wall City Jazz Band in Chester and I used to dep for Derek Vaux quite a bit because he was getting fed up with it. I was very pleased to play with them because they were the best trad band around. I was a builder at the time, restoring old cottages in North Wales, and I bought a farm in 1976. The mileage didn't bother me at all and I can't pretend that I found it a strain. I had a big estate car and the double-bass would fit comfortably into that. Nob was already doing Stanley Holloway narrations and I added some novelty songs, things by Flanders and Swann and Adge Cutler and the Wurzels. In 1982 I felt some things were going wrong and I left them rather than have it out with them. I did some depping for Robin Tankard, but I haven't done anything recently and I've now got a restaurant."

Pete Fryer (309) was a primary school headmaster: "I did find it difficult to fit my schedule around my school work and school used to get in the way sometimes. I had to put the school first as I was the headmaster, so there were occasions when the band came second. Even though teachers get good holidays, they didn't always come at the right time. For example, the band has been to Canada to play at the Chilliwack Festival and I couldn't go. The combination of jazz and teaching did have advantages as the parents booked the band for several good gigs, but some parents did not approve of the headmaster playing in a jazz band. I was also playing with the Brian Jones Big Band, but I had to give that up as there were so many demands upon my working life."

Talk of demanding jobs - a GP, John Higham, joined the Merseysippi Jazz Band in 1970 and I presumed that he must have missed a lot of gigs. **John Higham (310)**: "No, not at all. You can arrange your on-calls so that they don't clash with the gigs, and if they do, you can ask somebody to swop. A lot of doctors are quite happy to change duties with you as they will want you to do the same sometime. It never really clashed that much and it's certainly been good for me. If I was asked to give somebody the best piece of clinical advice I could give for staying well, I would tell them to get a creative hobby. I've come out to play at six o'clock at night, dog-tired at the end of the day, played for four hours and gone home feeling on top of the world. There's no real explanation for that."

But it all got too much for **John Parkes (311)**, who left the band in 1980: "I often look back and wonder how I endured those days. As well as all our dates at the Cavern, we frequently had to travel long distances overnight. I have a book of every date I played and I look at it now and wonder how I managed. When Dick stopped managing the band, I took over and I had to arrange the wages, the tax and the transport. I had to do this while I was running a busy shop selling fishing tackle. In the end, something had to go and

133

when somebody upset me, I left.   Perhaps it shouldn't have happened but I was tired out."

That was in 1980, shortly before the drummer **Pete Darwin (312)** wanted to join: "The bridge between me and the Merseys is John Higham, who was my GP in St Helens. John is a great guy, a good nut, a bloody good trumpet player and not a bad GP. He guested with a few bands that I had played with around St Helens and he was talking to me one day when I was in the doldrums. I was working in a labour club two nights a week and getting fed up with the bingo and that whole scene. I told him I was going nowhere and he said, 'Do you want to join the Merseys? Mike McCombe is moving to America, but you'll have to do an audition.' We went to Chaucer's Tavern and Mike McCombe asked me if I wanted to use his drums and I said, 'Yeah, if you don't mind.' He asked me who I played with and the names meant nothing to him. He asked me about my favourite bands and I said, 'There's only one British band that I never took much notice of and that was Ken Colyer's. I heard him for the first time at the Cavern and he was bloody great, but I've heard him four times since and I thought he was awful. I noticed that he never had a decent drummer with him.' Mike McCombe nearly swallowed his pipe and walked off to the bar without another word. I had put my foot right in it as Mike had played with Ken Colyer for two years. I didn't get the job but I'd played badly after that anyway. Another guy from Liverpool got the job but it wasn't his scene and he quit after three months. I got another visit from Dr John and he asked if I could play with the band on Thursday at the Nottingham Rhythm Club, and I said okay as it was a gig and not an audition. I immediately felt at one with the band and they asked me to join them. Most nights have been great. It is not the best jazz band in Britain by any means, but it is very good socially as they have all got good senses of humour."

George Melly

Wild Bill is both fiery and tender

By CHRISTOPHER LEE

THE contradictory Chicagoan cornet of Wild Bill Davison was heard to good advantage veering from fieriness towards tenderness at the Banyan Tree Club, Liverpool, last night.

Age has not diminished the uncompromising ferocity with which this 69-year-old jazzman attacks up-tempo vehicles, nor the emotional warmth which he brings to ballads.

The middle-of-the-road style of the Merseysippi Jazz Band suited him well. He slotted comfortably into the ensemble passages, and embarked on challenging solos which reflected confidence in his accompanists.

For a collection of ballads he was backed by the more modern Joe Palin Trio. Noteworthy performances included a reflective treatment of "Memories of You," followed by a punishingly fast but exhilerating " S'wonderful."

These two items in particular demonstrated the extremes of his musical c h a r a c t e r: Unashamed prettiness a n d scorching aggression. And in their different ways, each w a s equally satisfying.

DICK GOODWIN

LIVERPOOL

MERSEYSIPPI: mainstreamish and plenty of laughs

ONCE called "the greatest two-trumpet jazz band in the world," the Merseysippi Jazz Band, Liverpool's stalwart semi-pro outfit, are still keeping the jazz flag flying on the banks of the Mersey.

Reduced by one trumpeter —big Pete Daniels left the band when he moved to Manchester, though he still gigs occasionally—the band is still sticking to its 16-year-old policy of good swinging jazz, non-professional playing and lots of laughs.

Ex-bassist and now manager, Dick Goodwin told the

MM that, though there wasn't anywhere near as much work these days for jazz groups, they were still working regularly and accepting bookings away from their own once-a-week club.

The club meets each Sunday at the Cross Keys, a pub near Liverpool's Stadium. "We had offers of residency from a couple of places in Liverpool," said Dick. "But we were a bit disgusted the way a few places had thrown out jazz in favour of beat and we decided to go ahead and run the place ourselves.

"We also wanted to develop Sunday as a good night. We get on average between 70 and 90 people along. We have had as many as 180 and as few as 40 on a bad night.

"We don't make money out of it. By the time we've paid the band a few bob for playing we just about break even. But we've never been out for the money.

"In the early days, the money we got was very handy—it was useful to be paid a few nights a week for playing. But now we're all older and better established in our jobs so the money isn't nearly as important.

The Merseysippi have never fitted neatly into any jazz category. "I wish I knew what the band's musical policy was," said Dick. "We just play tunes we like in the way we like.

The band's line-up is: Don Lydiate (clarinet), Johnny Lawrence (trumpet/cornet), Johnny Parkes (trombone), Frank Robinson (piano), Ken Baldwin (guitar), Derek Baux (bass) and Tony Carter (drums).— A.W.

135

CHAPTER 9
OH, YOU CALIFORNIA
Sacramento Jazz Festivals

In the 1970s, John Stringer, a clarinet playing professor of metallurgy from Liverpool University, accepted a post in San Francisco. He knew the organising committee for the Sacramento Dixieland Jubilee, a jazz festival in California. He had taken an LP by the Merseysippi Jazz Band with him and as a result, the band was invited to play there. The invitation had come when the band was at a low ebb and it gave them a new lease of life, encouraging them to make new records.

Ken Baldwin (313): "When the festival started in 1974, there were 17 bands and when we first went in 1979, we were one of 70 bands. They thought it had got big enough, but now it is the largest jazz festival in the world with over 120 bands. It is getting a bit flabby as the venues are bus rides apart and may not even be in Sacramento. In the early days everyone played in Old Sacramento, which was like a cowboy town, and the venues were in bars and upstairs rooms. When we go now, we do 13 or 14 gigs in three or four days so we only get to see a handful of bands ourselves."

John Lawrence (314): "The festival started off with a few bands in California and as it was a success, the organisers brought in bands from Washington, New York and New Orleans. Then they started inviting jazz bands from overseas like ourselves and now they invite bands from as many foreign countries as they can find - Poland, Russia, Argentina, Japan - and it all goes down very well. People flock to see these bands, but there is something of the menagerie about it. They may come to see us for the same reason: can these guys from Liverpool play American jazz as well as the American bands?"

Kenny Ball (315): "I was talking to one of the organisers of the Sacramento Jazz Festival, and he said the Merseys were one of the most popular bands there, and of course they are great, a lovely band with a lovely sound. They've never changed their sound at all and they just swing along nicely. They are all terrific musicians and I must have known some of them for over 40 years."

If you see **John Higham (316)** on stage, you will see that, like Michael Jackson, he only wears one glove. "That dates from Sacramento in 1979 when I thought I had lost my trumpet. It had been carted off with another band's luggage, so I had to borrow a trumpet for the last session of the festival. We came back to San Francisco and I thought I'd buy another trumpet from a pawn shop and claim for it on the insurance. I got this super instrument, a Shilke, but it had lost all its silver from round the stops through the perspiration of the chap who had been playing it before. I asked, 'What is the best way of not having this happen again?' and the chap in the shop said, 'I would wear a little white glove. You can take it off and wash it, and that will absorb your perspiration without damaging your instrument.' So I got the nickname of Dr Strangeglove."

Don Lydiatt was asked by the organisers of the 1986 Sacramento Festival to join the World-Wide All- Stars, a band of the outstanding musicians at that year's festival. It was a considerable honour but there is quite a bit of mix and matching. **Don Lydiatt (317)**: "The committee would ask the top American musicians to play with bands in the festival. Johnny Guarnieri, a pianist who played with Artie Shaw, was allocated to us one year. He said, 'I want to do 'The World Is Waiting For The Sunrise'' and off he went. Then he did both 'Tiger Rag' and 'Maple Leaf Rag' in 5/4, which were difficult as we were adding an extra beat in each and every bar. At the end, he said, 'They're a nice bunch of guys but they talk funny.'"

Bob Ross (318): "The high spot of my time with the Merseys has to be playing with Dave McKenna's All Stars in Sacramento. There was Bob Wilbur, Nick Fatool, Dick Carey, Bob Havens and me. I was the only person in the band that I'd never heard of."

Frank Robinson (319): "I remember that session with Bob Ross very well as they were playing 'Lover' in five flats. It was going down in semitones all the time and I was glad it wasn't me. I was praying for it to go okay for him and he did very well."

Robin Tankard (320): "When we went to Sacramento, they said, 'Come on you limeys, do the Lambeth Walk.' It sounds very easy but it is very complicated but Clinton put his arms out and, in front of several thousand people, did the Lambeth Walk."

Mike McCombe (321): "Clinton goes down fine in England but there is no equivalent to his type of singing in the States and Americans don't know the old music hall songs that he does. He went down well in Sacramento, no doubt about that, but he's had better receptions in England."

Mike McCombe went with the MJB to Sacramento for four years. He befriended one of the workers at the festival, Barbara Barry. He moved to Sacramento, got divorced and married Barbara. Together they organised the appearances by the international bands. **Frank Robinson (322)**: "One year Mike McCombe did not apply for work permits. We had been there the previous year and he thought they would hold good. Somebody had found out that we hadn't applied for work permits and reported us. We were halfway through a session on Saturday when a lawman got us off the stand to complete application forms for the visas."

Since appearing at Sacramento, the Merseysippi's repertoire has developed in an unlikely way. **John Lawrence (323)**: "Originally it was called the Sacramento Dixieland Jubilee so you knew what to expect. It was all jazz, no pop or anything else, and each band was allocated a long set and told to take a break in the middle. If you've doing a two hour set, you can play for 45 minutes and then go off stage for half an hour, but you might lose the audience. We wondered how we were going to bridge the gap and Nob Baldwin said he'd do a monologue and it was one of the Stanley Holloway ones, 'Albert And The Lion', and it brought the house down. We played 16 times in four days and the Americans kept asking him to do 'Alvin And The Lion' (sic) again. It has become a tradition now that if we need a break, Nob will do a monologue and he has done 'Albert And The Lion', 'The Battle of Hastings' and several others with great success. When we had half an hour to spare at the end of one of our recording sessions, we asked him to record them. We put them on the 'Happy Hour' cassette and they go very well with the party tunes."

Ken Baldwin (324): "I heard Stanley Holloway do the monologues in my youth and I found the books with them in and learnt them when I was about 15 or 16 at the Collegiate. To this day I can repeat a dozen, and by the time I forget them, it will be time to pack up doing anything. I like doing them in the States because the

Americans are mystified. They hear 'The Battle Of Hastings' and they can't understand half of it. They don't know about William the Conqueror, but they understand bits of the monologue of course."

Robin Tankard (325): "Our worst night was when we had to drink vodka with the Russians in Sacramento. The Americans were so shy at the time - glasnost was just starting - and they thought they would get the British band to welcome the Russians. Because of flight delays, they turned up late and they had no money and no food. They only had cases of vodka and we made a terrible mistake and drank it with them. The next morning we were playing in an old folks' home and that was our worst-ever gig. We were appalling. Nob was rolling on the floor and I said, 'What are you doing?', and he said, 'I've lost my plectrum', and he took his shoes and socks off and found it in his shoe. The old folks were looking at us as though we should be booked in immediately."

The Merseys sometimes extended their visit with other engagements. **Frank Robinson (326)**: "Lu Watters had played in the Dawn Club in San Francisco, so we were very pleased to be playing there. We couldn't advertise the fact because our permits had run out. We put up some other name on the billing because we risked being deported."

Pete Fryer (327): "The Sacramento festival used to fall roughly in line with the Whit holiday at school, and I can remember coming back from my first time on a Saturday in 1981. On the Monday morning, I was going in to teach and I was jet lagged. I knew the term, but I didn't realise what it meant until I experienced it. It was weird and I was falling asleep over the children's work. I needed three or four days to get over it and be part of the living world again."

John Higham (328). "We came back on a high from Sacramento in 1982 and then we played this pub in Skipton where nobody turned up, not a single person. It wasn't our fault. The manager had forgotten to advertise us so nobody knew it was on. It was quite a comedown for us."

MJB Audience at Sacramento

Clinton in Sacramento

Jan Sutherland

MERSEYSIPPI JAZZ BAND
From Liverpool, England

At The GREAT 1995 CONNECTICUT TRADITIONAL JAZZ FESTIVAL

SUNRISE RESORT

MOODUS, CONNECTICUT

TENT #2, 12:00-1:00 PM, SAT. AUGUST 5, 1995

MUSICIANS: BOB BALDWIN (Banjo, Leader), JOHN HIGHAM (Trumpet), JOHN LAWRENCE (Cornet), PETE FRYER (Trombone), DAVE THOMAS (Clarinet), FRANK ROBINSON (Piano), ROBIN TANKARD (Bass), PETE DARWIN (Drums)

MJB with Jan Sutherland

CHAPTER 10
CLOSING TIME?
Hartley's - Aigburth Arms - Crowne Plaza - Today's repertoire

I

The Merseysippi Jazz Band's career has been a roller-coaster ride. Although some of the residencies may be lows, they have been balanced by such events as the Sacramento Jazz Festival. In 1984 their residencies took a marked step upwards via their Monday nights at Hartley's Wine Bar at the Albert Dock. **Pete Fryer (329)**: "We had been playing at a pub in Hardman Street near the Phil called Chaucer's Tavern. It was small but it was good to play there. They pushed us upstairs when they were decorating, which wasn't nearly as good. Support started to fade away and so we were looking for somewhere else. It was 1984, the year of the Garden Festival, and Tony Davis got together the Reds and Blues Marching Band, comprised of the Merseys, the Blue Mags and a few others, and we did a lot of work there, usually on a Sunday. In line with this, they were refurbishing the Albert Dock and when we heard of Hartley's, we invited the managers to hear us. We had started at the rebuilt Cavern, but that never got going for us and we moved to Hartley's. On the first night, it was jammed to the door and the managers were tickled pink."

The Merseysippi Jazz Band welcomed many guests to Hartley's including Russia's Igor Bourco's Uralsky Jazzmen and, from America, the Paradise City Jazz Band and the South 'Frisco Jazz Band. The countless musicians who have been pleased to guest with the band include Alan Barnes, Campbell Burnap, Mike Cotton, Digby Fairweather, Dave Mott, Roger Myerscough, Keith Nichols, Dave Shepherd, Johnny Richardson, Pete Strange, Roy Williams and John Barnes. **John Barnes (330)**: "I am an honorary life member of the Merseys and I may be the only one. It's probably because I bought them a round. I think music keeps you young. It certainly keeps your mind going because even if you don't read music very well, you're improvising. A lot of the audience think that we are just standing there and looking at them and thinking, 'She's pretty', but of course we have got a million things going through our heads improvising on the chord sequence of the tunes we are playing. You can't relax and as you long as you don't drink too

142

much and do some exercise, swimming or something, you can go on for a hell of a time."

The audiences are amused by their microphone stands with attached pint glass holders. **Pete Darwin (331)**: "When they came out, I thought it would be a good idea to get one for myself. I stuck it on one of my cymbal stands, and they all said, 'Hey, where did you get that?'. Next thing, everyone in the band had one. Good ol' Nob always manages to kick a pint of beer over. If you put a pint of beer on the floor within a yard of him, he'll kick it over. Sometimes it happens two or three times on a gig. We put one on his guitar-stand so that his beer was elevated from the floor by two feet, which seemed a great idea, but he started kicking the stand over and it was back to square one. He gave his stand to his son. We get a lot of people asking where they can get the holders, so beer and jazz do go together."

Frank Robinson (332): "Hartley's turned out to be the longest residency we ever had: at 15 years it is twice as long as anywhere else. We found that a lot of our audience were around in the Temple days: they'd got married, their children have left and suddenly they were free to do what they liked and they came back to us."

Tony Barrow (333): "I returned to listen to the Merseys in Hartley's and it was one of the most pleasantly nostalgic evenings I have enjoyed for a very long time."

Alan Sytner (334): "The Merseys are a terrific bunch and I always have great fun with them. Whenever I see them, we have an absolute ball. They are a miracle and they are amazing and it shows you that alcohol is a very good preservative."

Derek Vaux (335): "There are a lot of jazz bands in Liverpool and in the country, but jazz is not a widely popular music. When I came back to the Merseys in 1997, I thought the place was going to be full of young people and I was staggered to see people with blue rinses and on Zimmer frames: the audience had grown old, like us. I'd like jazz to become popular again but most of the musicians in the city are in their 50s and 60s, the guitarist Gary Potter being an exception."

143

A comparison can be made with the Spinners. **John Lawrence (336)**: "When we started playing, we used to play to an audience of serious jazz enthusiasts and collectors, who took it very seriously, but that has changed. We now play to an audience that just wants to have an enjoyable evening. They won't get that if we play obscure New Orleans songs, so we have got to make it enjoyable with the compèring, the fooling around and the jokes. It's completely different from the way we started."

Also similar to the Spinners link are their coloured shirts. **Ken Baldwin (337)**: "I publish a list of the gigs that the band is doing in the forseeable future and at the bottom of it, I put down the shirts that we will wear. We have ten different colours and on occasion I have picked the wrong one, and I'm supposed to be the guy who is telling the others what to put on."

Pete Fryer (338): "I had been cleaning out my trombone at home. I put it back in the case, put it in the car and went off to Hartleys. After I'd left, one of my daughters had gone into the kitchen and found my trombone slide on the hob. I arrived at Hartleys and I was flabbergasted when about 15 minutes later, John Lawrence walked in carrying my trombone slide. He said, 'You might find a use for this.' My wife Pat had phoned John, told him what had happened and then taken it round to him."

Drummer **Pete Darwin (339)** owns a musical instrument shop in St Helens.: "The rep came in from Gibson guitars and they make a lot of accessories for different things, not just guitars but educational things too. He had these quail calls, which were normally £8 but the price had dropped to 90p as a special offer. I bought a couple as I knew what I could do with them. When they arrived in the post, I found that they were long brass poles with bulbs on and when you pressed the bulb, they went 'Eek, eek, eek'. Great sound. I took them along to a gig and gave one to the bass player, Robin Tankard. In the middle of a bluesy 'Do You Know What It Means To Miss New Orleans?', our clarinet player Don Lydiatt started playing this beautiful solo and all of a sudden, he heard 'Eek, eek, eek'. He stopped playing and looked at his clarinet. All the band thought it was the reed on his clarinet. He started blowing again, 'Eek, eek, eek'. I couldn't stop laughing and Robin had his head behind the bass and was doubled up too. It slowly dawned on them that it was us. The quail calls got thrown in the Mersey and one day I'll follow them."

Or again. **Pete Darwin (340)**: "Nob Baldwin got up one night to sing 'When Somebody Thinks You're Wonderful' and Derek and I had motor horns behind him. Everybody was laughing but Nob wasn't laughing at all. He said, 'Right, you chaps, enough's enough. This is not a circus, it is a jazz band.' The head boy had spoken so we put them away and carried on playing."

With a new management that showed little interest in jazz, Hartley's residency ended in 1999, ironically the year of their 50th birthday celebrations. Undeterred, they switched to another pub in the Albert Dock, the J Bar, later Bar Monaco, but in September 2000, they moved four miles out of the city to the Aigburth Arms in Aigburth Vale. The main room can comfortably take 100 patrons and the acoustics are okay. To quote Frank Robinson, "The Aigburth Arms is fine and I hope they keep us here."

II

With only Pete Darwin working full-time, the members of the Merseysippi Jazz Band have become, in their retirement, professionals. For bookings when Pete Darwin isn't available, Trevor Carlisle returns on drums. Because they have more time available, the Merseys often play outside Liverpool at jazz clubs and festivals.

Jim Caine (341): "I first came across the Merseys in the Isle of Man. We had a jazz record club of which I was a founder member and we used to meet regularly and play records. We never thought of putting live groups on but then in 1972, a gentleman who is now the Chairman of the Manx Jazz Club, Alan Grubb, brought the Merseys over on his own initiative. The record club decided to support it and it was then that we decided to form our own jazz club. The Merseys were our first band and they have been over countless times since then. We look upon them as our band."

Alan Grubb (342): "There was no jazz on the Isle of Man until Nat Gonella came in June 1972 to play the Gaiety Theatre, and the MJB and Bruce Turner were also on the bill. I repeated the concert in August and they were two great concerts. In 1974 we had a riot of a concert with the MJB and George Melly at the Laxey Glen Ballroom. Then we had George Chisholm and the MJB at the Majestic Hotel, Onchan. George was in 'The Black And White Minstrel Show' on BBC-TV at the time, and around 450 people turned up, so that was another great night. We also had Bud Freeman and Humphrey Lyttelton with the MJB and some more gigs with George Chisholm. We had our first jazz festival in 1993 and the MJB played five festivals on the trot. I particularly remember the third festival as they met up with Nat Gonella again. He was 87 and had long given up the trumpet but he sang with them each night."

Howard Nicholson (343) of the Ongar Jazz Club in Essex: "I think people always appreciate Liverpool people for their humour and so many comedians come from the city. The Merseys are full of humour. They present themselves in a nice, light humorous way and you can tell that they enjoy their music."

Robin Tankard (344): "Some years ago I was doing a broadcast for Radio 2 with the Merseys in Cork and there was this guy with a trilby and we had a drink together. He said he was playing with a band at the festival and afterwards there were several young girls who said that I'd been talking to Van Morrison. Pardon my ignorance, but he was very nice."

Derek Vaux (345): "People go on about the conditions at Glastonbury, but I'm sure we've played worse. One Saturday in torrential rain at Upton Upon Severn in 1998, we were in the Armstrong tent and it was absolutely packed and it was wonderful. The bar was a quarter of a mile away across water and mud, and we played for three hours and drank nothing at all except Fanta orange. Amazingly, we played pretty well and we made up for it afterwards by getting off the site and finding a pub." (On the Upton ticket, the admission price was described as 'ADM': Derek told John Higham that it stood for 'Ankle Deep in Mud'.")

Pete Fryer (346): "I'll never forget that day as the main festival site was on a huge meadow and this meadow was like a quagmire. The cars were getting stuck and they had a gang of people pushing them out. We had to paddle through the mud to get to the stage and I hated going on stage with terribly dirty shoes. I am very particular about my shiny shoes. When we have been to Sacramento, I have roomed with Frank Parr, and in the morning I would get up early to polish my shoes and he would pull my leg something terrible about that. The others tease me about it too."

Noel Walker (347): "I can't say that I've followed the Merseys through their career, although I do hear Humph play their tracks now and again on Radio 2, so I have been keeping up with that lovely two trumpet sound which is unique in English jazz. Think of how many two trumpet bands there were - there was one in Bristol many years ago. When I was a kid, I was a traddie and I thought the Merseys were a very modern band. I heard them for the first time in a long time some weeks ago in London and it was lovely to hear that mellow two-trumpet sound and lovely to meet some of the guys that I had known from so many years before. They are still enthusiastic, perhaps not playing with the fire that they had when they were much younger, but then who has got the fire 50 years on?"

Mike McCombe (348): "The Merseys still sound the same to me. If I'd walked in blindfold tonight, I would still know who was playing. There are a lot of two horn bands in America but there are very few in England. Most of the American two horn bands have a tuba. Here it is a string bass, which makes a very big difference to the sound of the band and is very distinctive."

The Merseysippi Jazz Band held a special party for its golden jubilee in February 1999 and booked the new Crowne Plaza Hotel, which is next to the Royal Liver Building, for a weekend of jazz. Over 600 people attended the celebrations and it was such a success that they arranged the Merseyside Jazz Festival 2000, also at the Crowne Plaza, a year later. This featured the key bands on Merseyside together with several bands and guest musicians from outside the area. This in turn led to another festival in 2001 and it looks as though the Merseys, despite their advancing years, are left with organising an annual festival. They must be sorry that they didn't think of it ten years earlier.

George Melly (349): "The Merseys are a miracle: they have been playing longer than anybody else, they have always played well and they haven't altered a bit. It is always lovely to hear them and they are very, very nice people, and they rode out the whole Liverpool beat scene. They were outside the Palm House in Sefton Park when I went to make a speech to say how marvellous it was that they were restoring this monument in its full Edwardian magnificence."

Humphrey Lyttelton (350): "The Merseysippi Jazz Band is an institution and they are all mates as well. I think it is a fine band and they wouldn't have lasted this long if they were duff. They play things right and as they've recorded one of my tunes, they get Brownie points for that as well." (Two actually, Humph - 'Hop Frog' and 'Bad Penny Blues'.)

III

Does the band practice individually? **John Lawrence (351)**: "Do I heck? They say, 'If you miss a day's practice, you notice it. If you miss two days' practice, the band notices it, and if you miss three days', the audience notices it.' I practice when I can and when I feel inclined but it is terribly boring. It's no good picking up a horn and playing one or two tunes that you like to play. The American trumpet player Freddie Hubbard said the only way to practice is to practice the tunes that you can't play, which is worse than playing scales. I should practice more as I don't want my lip to go."

Ken Baldwin (352): "Some bands do two or three choruses, solos round the front line, and then two choruses out. We are always doing little duets and codas to make the numbers more interesting, but we don't rehearse much anymore. We used to rehearse every Monday night and now it is every three months."

Pete Fryer (353): "I have always liked the Lu Watters' tune, 'I'm Going Hunting' and I wanted a full band rehearsal on it. We didn't have one but we tried it out on the audience last night and it went all right. It often works like that. If you have a residency, you can play tunes that you haven't done before and the audience will let you off if it isn't quite right. We know what we're doing, but it can get tricky with a four-piece front line. We should be working out our harmonies in private first. You'll see us communicating while we're playing a number so we know who's taking the next solo."

Derek Vaux (354): "The band has such an enormous repertoire and we never have a set programme. We might in extremis write down a few tunes in the pub beforehand but in the end the band has got such a wide range of styles and sounds that we play it by ear, depending on the audience reaction we are getting. If people want to hear New Orleans jazz, it is no good playing a load of Ellington stuff. The band can very easily assess the reaction by the things they play first."

John Lawrence (355): "Many tunes that King Oliver and Louis Armstrong played are still being played by us, but we have added a lot more from other sources. We haven't got bogged down with one particular repertoire. We have between 300 and 400 songs that we can play without previous preparation. A lot of them are standards, but we like to feel that the way we play the tune is a little bit more important than the actual tune itself. 'Jersey Lightning' was written in the 20s and we are still playing it because it is a good tune and we can make it swing. Any band including ours plays it a little differently from the last time, so there is no reason why we should stop playing the tune."

John Barnes (356): "Once they've played the theme, they pass the solos around and sometimes they forget that I don't know all their repertoire. They say, 'Here we go', and I've had to stumble along on tunes I don't know. Luckily I've got pretty good ears and once I've played a couple of choruses I have more or less got it. There is a lot of improvisation, they don't get hold of sheet music and read it, they do their arrangements by ear. They get a good recording of a tune and they work it out from that."

Keith Nichols (357), who plays piano, trombone and soprano sax in the Cotton Club Orchestra, sometimes guests with the Merseys: "I am a fairly recent fan and friend of theirs and I love doing spots with them. I write for EMI's music library and one day I was writing a piece in the style of Lu Watters and the Yerba Buena Band. As I was doing it, I thought that it would be nice to dedicate to them. I called it 'Minstrels Of Annie Street' and I was very pleased that they liked it and included it in their repertoire. I brought my own band to the Crowne Plaza and I played it as a tribute to them."

Dennis Gracey (358): "The band's repertoire has changed

tremendously. They have play a lot of tunes that I'm not familiar with. It is the right way to go as it does relieve any boredom that might be there. A lot of bands get hooked on what the audiences want the bands to play and so they end up playing the same requests every week and get into a rut."

Tony Davis (359): "The Merseys haven't stood still at all. They have kept a freshness in their playing which is incredible. A lot of the stuff is their old repertoire, but they are always adding new tunes. They've just played 'Smoky Mokes' which is one of the first tunes I've heard them play, and now they've added 'Cleopatra's Blues', which Roger Higham, John's brother, dug out."

John Higham (360): "I am the bane of their lives. Don goes, 'Not another new song' as he thinks we have a large enough repertoire as it is. I like the challenge of finding a number that very few people perform and making our arrangement of it. It is very satisfying when you get it right. One that I can't get past the band veto is 'Lips That Touched Kippers Will Never Touch Mine', which was written in 1924. Despite the title, it is a very good song."

Ted Baker (361): "The Merseys play a lot of standards but they throw in humorous songs as well, which is great for the audiences. I love it when Clint is with them because he is so visual."

Clinton Ford (362): "My hair has been this colour for 30 years and I used to stand out in a crowd. Now I get lost. Looking around the room today, it's like being in the Alps."

Jim Caine (363): "I love the enthusiasm they display and the vigour for the music especially when you consider the average age of the members of the band. George Chisholm was guesting with us one time and when the band came back on, he said, 'Here they come, the boys, ha, ha, ha. This band is so old that they have to carry their own doctor with them.' They know each other so well and play to each other's strengths. Individually they are good musicians but put them together and they are a really good cracking band."

George Melly (364) believes that you can retain your following with age: "The English worship the old, especially if they are doing something inappropriate like breaking the ice on the Serpentine on

New Year's Day. To be honest, it is fairly grotesque for me to be singing about sensual activities now I'm 70, but people seem to like it."

Pete Fryer (365): "Some of the guys are getting on a bit but you wouldn't know it, because playing jazz keeps your brain busy and keeps you young. I'm one of the younger members at 58 and Pete Darwin is slightly younger than me. I'm staying with this band, no doubt about it. They are never going to get rid of me. They've never sacked anyone so I'm fairly secure there."

The Merseysippi Jazz Band has lost past members - Pete Daniels died in 1988 and Dick Goodwin in 1996 - but the band continues and mercifully, no one even has hearing difficulties like George Melly. **Derek Vaux (366)**: "It is a dangerous claim to make but I believe the Merseysippi Jazz Band is the oldest two trumpet jazz band in the world. We've only known about jazz since the turn of the 20th century so the Merseys have been around for half the history of what has become known as jazz. Humph has done 50 as a bandleader, which is incredible, but then he hasn't got four original members in his band."

John Lawrence (367) looks far younger than his years and could play the lead in the Cecil Parkinson story: "From time to time, someone will say as we are packing up, 'Whoever would have thought it?' and I'll know exactly what he means. Whoever would have thought that we'd be playing 50 years later? We never planned the future, we were just eight guys who enjoyed playing music and we'll be going on for as long as it takes."

John Higham (368): "Wild Bill Davison went right on to the end and was still playing well. Clarinet players can often go on longer than trumpet players. Four of the band are around 75 now so it can't go on for much longer and I don't know what I'll do then. I do dep with other bands and enjoy that but nothing compares to the Merseys."

May this book draw to a close and end with a full stop long before the Merseys do.

*30th Birthday
Ticket*

*35th Birthday
Ticket*

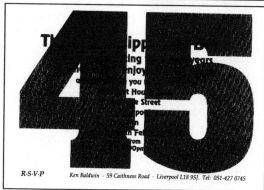

*45th Birthday
Ticket*

*Golden Jubilee
Ticket*

35 — and still stomping

EIGHT jazz freaks and their friends foot-stomped their way through a special birth-day celebration in Liverpool at the weekend.

The popular Merseysippi Jazz Band is now 35 years old, and still has two of its origi-nal members.

Pianist Frank Robin-son and banjo player Nob Baldwin were there at the start in 1949.

The band members, who now have a regular Monday night spot at Chaucers, in the city, have never tired of playing their kind of music together.

Security

"In the fifties we had the chance of turning professional. But by staying amateur we had the best of both worlds. We've had the security of our jobs, and we've been able to enjoy our music," said Frank.

Jazz is still very popu-lar, though their audi-ence has tended to grow up with the group

The group has travelled to America playing its special kind of Lu Watters-style jazz.

Long-time fan Brian Linford, a confectioner in Aigburth, baked a big birthday cake — in the shape of a double bass — for the celebra-tion.

Many happy returns . . . Confectioner Brian Linford shows members of the Merseysippi jazz band the cake he baked for the celebration;

Isle of Man, 1999
Back row (L to R) Pete Darwin, John Lawrence, Ken Baldwin,
Pete Fryer, John Higham.
Front row (L to R) Derek Vaux, Don Lydiatt, Frank Robinson

NOTES ON CONTRIBUTORS

The numbered paragraphs relate to taped interviews with myself, mostly conducted between 1998 and 2001. Some selections have been broadcast on BBC Radio Merseyside's 'On The Beat', but otherwise they are unique to this publication.

Connie Atkinson (1) (3) has edited blues magazines in New Orleans and completed a degree at the Institute of Popular Music in Liverpool.

Bob Azurdia (183) was a Liverpool journalist who joined BBC Radio Merseyside when it opened in 1967.

The trumpet player **Kenny Baker (40)** was best known for his work on the TV series, 'The Beiderbecke Affair'.

Ted Baker (361) is a jazz photographer.

Ken Baldwin (4) (71) (77) (80) (81) (83) (87) (95) (99) (103) (117) (132) (152) (162) (165) (170) (199) (219) (223) (235) (248) (266) (276) (280) (285) (287) (294) (313) (324) (337) (352) plays banjo and guitar and is a founder member of the Merseysippi Jazz Band.

Kenny Ball (19) (32) (36) (42) (52) (121) (127) (256) (265) (315) led the most commercially successful Trad band, even making the US Top 10 with "Midnight In Moscow".

Even now, in his seventies, **Chris Barber (25) (53) (57) (97) (126) (237) (257)** is constantly on the road with his Jazz And Blues Band

Manchester-born **John Barnes (129) (330) (356)** has played clarinet and saxophone with most of the top British jazz musicians including 12 years with Humph.

Tony Barrow (138) (282) (333) worked as a publicist for NEMS Enterprises from 1963 to 1968 and had the Beatles amongst his clients. He started by managing the Mike McCombe Skiffle Group.

Roger Baskerfield (189) was part of the Coney Island Skiffle Group.

Clarinet player **Acker Bilk (28)** has had both jazz ('Buona Sera') and MOR hits ('Stranger On The Shore').

Terry Birkinhead (7) (9) leads the umbrella parades on Merseyside.

The drummer **Tony Brown (279) (302)** has depped with the Merseys on occasion.

Jim Caine (341) (363) is a pianist and broadcaster on Manx Radio.

Trevor Carlisle (142) (156) (158) (169) played drums with the MJB for ten years and still deps occasionally today.

John Chilton (13) (14) (45) (264) is a jazz historian who also plays trumpet and leads the Feetwarmers.

Harold Culling (67) (69) (72) (113) was the most ardent jazz record collector on Merseyside.

Pete Darwin (312) (331) (339) (340) has played drums with the MJB since 1982.

Tony Davis (2) (8) (227) (359) ran the Gin Mill Skiffle Group, which transmogrified into the highly successful folk-singing group, the Spinners. He now presents his own programme on Jazz FM.

Valerie Dicks (198) (263) was a regular at the Cavern.

Ralph Ellis (247) played lead guitar for the Swinging Blue Jeans.

Ray Ennis (209) is the leader and lead singer of the Swinging Blue Jeans.

Clinton Ford (215) (216) (217) (222) (267) (268) (295) (362) has sung with the Merseys on and off since 1957. Still in excellent voice but he looks so like Colonel Sanders that you're tempted to give him your chicken-in-a-basket orders.

Pete Fryer (212) (309) (327) (329) (338) (346) (353) (365) plays trombone for the MJB.

Jim Godbolt (55) has been involved in the management and agency bookings of many UK jazz groups. His memoirs, 'All This And 10%' (Robert Hale, 1976) and 'All This And Many A Dog' (Quartet, 1986), are a close second to George Melly's.

Bob Gough (75) (89) (93) (166) was a member of the Wallasey Rhythm Club and now plays piano for Bob Dwyer's Hot Seven in the London area.

Dennis Gracey (68) (73) (76) (84) (90) (94) (108) (306) (358) was the MJB's first trombone player.

Alan Grubb (342) is the chairman of the Manx Jazz Club.

Pat Halcox (273) plays trumpet for Chris Barber's Jazz Band.

Colin Hanton (204) played drums with John Lennon's Quarry Men.

Les Harris (30) plays trumpet for the Blue Magnolia Jazz Orchestra.

Bill Harry (243) was at the Liverpool College of Art with John Lennon and Stuart Sutcliffe and became the editor of the 'Mersey Beat' newspaper.

Keith Hemmings (179) (190) is an architect involved in the initial stages of the Cavern and whose son, Paul, plays in Lightning Seeds.

Dr **John Higham (29) (31) (37) (38) (41) (98) (153) (284) (310) (316) (328) (360) (368)** plays trumpet for the Merseysippi Jazz Band.

Hil Hughes (252) is one of Liverpool's best jazz singers and the sister of Tommy Hughes.

Tommy Hughes (131) was a founder member of the Swinging Blue Jeans.

To all but the pedantic, cornet player **John Lawrence (18) (21) (24) (26) (27) (34) (47) (64) (70) (74) (85) (104) (109) (111) (112) (114)**

(119) (120) (122) (125) (128) (133) (141) (144) (146) (149) (161) (168) (174) (181) (191) (228) (229) (230) (231) (233) (236) (241) (242) (251) (270) (272) (283) (286) (293) (296) (303) (305) (314) (323) (336) (351) (355) (367) is a founder member of the Merseysippi Jazz Band.

Brian Linford (134) (140) (195) (260) (277) was the manager of the Mardi Gras.

Don Lydiatt (62) (96) (106) (115) (118) (123) (130) (155) (186) (193) (249) (250) (255) (271) (278) (281) (298) (304) (307) (317) plays clarinet for the MJB.

Endlessly creative even at 80 years old (he has just recorded with Radiohead!), trumpet player **Humphrey Lyttelton (17) (20) (33) (35) (46) (56) (232) (274) (350)** has inspired generations of British jazz musicians.

Mike McCombe (214) (254) (290) (292) (299) (300) (321) (348) had 15 years in the MJB's engine room.

John McCormick (137) (160) is a jazz musician who also played double-bass with the Spinners for many years.

Ray McFall (246) became the owner of the Cavern in 1959.

Ross McManus (91) (102) played trumpet in a modern jazz group in Liverpool and then joined Joe Loss and his Orchestra as a vocalist. He is Elvis Costello's father.

Alf Mellor (167), a bluegrass musician, followed the MJB in their early years.

Liverpool singer and art critic, **George Melly (10) (12) (23) (43) (60) (92) (238) (258) (275) (349) (364)** sang first with Mick Mulligan's Magnolia Jazz Band and then with John Chilton's Feetwarmers.

Keith Nichols (357) runs the Cotton Club Orchestra.

Howard Nicholson (343) runs the Ongar Jazz Club in Essex.

John 'Archie' Parkes (54) (58) (210) (211) (225) (245) (261) (269) (291) (311) played trombone for the Merseys for 23 years.

Frank Parr (63) (110) (154) (171) (173) (239) combined county cricket with trombone playing in the Merseys.

Sonny Phillips (105) led the Dusty Hat Band for many years and plays country music around Liverpool's clubs and pubs. His brother, Terry Phillips, was Mr Universe and also owned the Wooky Hollow.

A superb raconteur, the London agent and manager **Ken Pitt (51)** wrote a book about his most famous client, 'David Bowie - The Pitt Report' (Design, 1983).

Merseyside trumpet player **Roy Potts (16)** leads the Five And A Penny Jazz Band

Frank Robinson (6) (44) (79) (82) (86) (88) (101) (107) (116) (136) (145) (148) (150) (157) (192) (218) (226) (240) (319) (322) (326) (332) plays piano and is a founder member of the Merseysippi Jazz Band.

Harold Rosen (151) was a key promoter of jazz in Liverpool.

Bob Ross (308) (318) started depping for Derek Vaux on the double-bass in the 1970s and wound up as a regular member.

Saxophonist **Ronnie Scott (59) (61)** founded his world-famous jazz club in London in 1959.

In the 1950s **Monty Sunshine (11)** played clarinet with Chris Barber's Jazz Band and then formed his own band.

Alan Sytner (100) (143) (175) (176) (177) (178) (180) (182) (184) (185) (187) (196) (197) (200) (201) (203) (206) (244) (259) (334) was the founder and first owner of the Cavern.

Robin Tankard (15) (22) (48) (320) (325) (344) played double-bass with the Merseys from 1982 to 1997 and now plays with Roy Potts' Five And A Penny Jazz Band

Phil Taylor (49) (288) (289) (297) is one of the MJB's long-standing fans.

As you might expect, **Alf Tweedle (253)** was the leader of Alf Tweedle's Dixielanders.

Derek Vaux (5) (50) (221) (301) (335) (345) (354) (366) is enjoying his second stint of playing double-bass for the Merseysippi Jazz Band. Over the years he has also worked with Ken Colyer, Bobby Mickleburgh, Ken Sims and Bob Wallis. He has thrown his double-bass around in Dr Crock's Crackpot Eleven and accompanied Ella Fitzgerald on TV.

Since 1957, **Steve Voce (124) (159) (164) (194) (202) (205) (207) (208) (234)** has written a controversial column in 'Jazz Journal' while his 'Jazz Panorama' has been broadcast for over 30 years on BBC Radio Merseyside.

Noel Walker (39) (213) (220) (347) led the Noel Walker Stompers and then became a record producer, having huge success with the Fortunes.

Ralph 'Bags' Watmough (65) (66) (78) (135) (188) (262) formed his first band in Crosby in 1948. It disbanded in 1965 and one of its long-standing members was John Higham's brother, Roger. Bags Watmough was called Bugs Mouthwash by Bruce Turner.

Dave Williams (139) (147) (172) (224) was a jazz fan in the 1950s and still is. He is the chairman of BBC Radio Merseyside's listening panel.

Manchester-born trombone player **Roy Williams (163)** has played with most of the top UK jazz musicians including 13 years with Alex Welsh.

Frank Robinson now

Frank Robinson then

160

APPENDIX 1

THE MERSEYSIPPI JAZZ BAND - PERSONNEL

Trumpet
> Wally Fisher (1949 - 1950)
> Pete Daniels (1952 - 1970)
> John Higham (1970 - today)

Cornet
> John Lawrence (1950 - today)

Trombone
> Dennis Gracey (1949 - 1950)
> Frank Parr (1950 - 1956)
> John Haworth (1956 - 1957)
> John 'Archie' Parkes (1957 - 1980)
> Pete Fryer (1980 - today)
> *Briefly: Ian Ashworth, Ken Horton, Alf Jones, Harry Price, John Rubin.*

Clarinet
> Pat Evans (real name:Evan Patrick) (Feb 1949 - Sept 1949)
> Don Lydiatt (Oct 1949 - today)

Piano
> Frank Robinson (1949 - today)

Banjo / Guitar
> Ken 'Nob' Baldwin (1949 - today)

Double-bass
> Dick Goodwin (1949 - 1964)
> Derek Vaux (1964 - 1974) (also played tuba, briefly)
> Derek Vaux and Bob Ross (1974 - 1977)
> Bob Ross (1977 - 1982)
> Robin Tankard (1982 - 1997) (also played tuba)
> Derek Vaux (1997 - today)

Drums

> Ken Metcalfe (1949 - 1950)
> Ken Tinkler (1950)
> George Bennett (1950 - 1954)
> Trevor Carlisle (1954 - 1964)
> Tony Carter, Tony Crofts, Aynsley Dunbar,
> Mike Holmes, Noddy Noble, Brian Roberts (1964 - 1967)
> Mike McCombe (1967 - 1982)
> Bobby Boyd (1982)
> Pete Darwin (1982 - today)
> *Briefly: Tony Brown, Alan Critchley, Tommy Davis,*
> *Bill Dennett, John Fogg,*
> *Rob Foster, Mike Holmes, Lenny Lister, Ken London,*
> *John May, Don Morris, P.J. Pratley,*
> *Bill Rimmer and someone called Clive.*

Male Vocalist

> Clinton Ford (1957 and occasionally ever since)

Female Vocalists

> Jill Martin (1958 - 1977)
> Jan Sutherland (1977 - 1982)
> *Briefly: Val Barlow, Julie Dennis, Edna Gallagher,*
> *Pam Peters*

Honorary Life Members

> *John Barnes (leading UK musician),*
> *Leon Oakley and Vince Saunders (both of the South 'Frisco*
> *Jazz Band)*
> *Eric Holroyd (Bradford-born musician who has lived in*
> *Australia for 35 years and plays in the 10th Avenue Jazz*
> *Band)*

John Lawrence
with Jill Martin

162

APPENDIX 2

THE MERSEYSIPPI JAZZ BAND - VENUES

Residencies:

Weaver's Café, New Brighton (1948)
Sunset Café, New Brighton (1948)
Hotel Victoria, New Brighton (1948 - 1949)
Tick-Tock Café, New Brighton (1949)

Tudor Restaurant, Liverpool (1950)
Mayfair Restaurant, Liverpool (1950)
Temple Restaurant, Victoria Street, Liverpool (1950 - 1951)
St George's Restaurant, Liverpool (1951)
Britannia Restaurant, Liverpool (1952)
Washington Hotel, Liverpool (1952)
Temple Restaurant, Victoria Street, Liverpool (1953 - 1957)
Cavern Club, Mathew Street, Liverpool (1957 - 1959)
Mardi Gras Club, Mount Pleasant, Liverpool (1959 - 1964)

Cross Keys, Edmund Street, Liverpool (1964 -1966)
Four Winds Club, Liverpool (1964)
Temple Restaurant, Victoria Street, Liverpool (1966)
Cross Keys, Edmund Street, Liverpool (1967 -1968)
Club Ebony, Southport (1967)
Magic Lantern, Birkenhead (1967 - 1968)
1250 Club, Liverpool (1967)
Golden Goblet, Liverpool (1968)
Central Hotel, Widnes (1968)
Tudor Restaurant, New Brighton (1969)
Bier Keller, Liverpool (1969)

The Sportsman, Liverpool (1971 - 1977)
The Harrow, Culcheth (1972)
Flintlock Club, Liverpool (1974)
The Swan, Liverpool (1977)
Chaucer's Tavern, Hardman Street, Liverpool (1977 - 1984)

The Cumberland, Liverpool (1982 - 1983)
Cavern Club, Mathew Street, Liverpool (1984)

Hartley's Wine Bar, Albert Dock, Liverpool (1984 - 1999)
J Bar (later Bar Monaco), Albert Dock, Liverpool (1999 - 2000)

New York Café Bar, Mossley Hill, Liverpool (2000)
Aigburth Arms, Aigburth, Liverpool (2000 - today)

Notable festival appearances:

First Liverpool Jazz Festival, Cavern, Liverpool (1960)

Sacramento Dixieland Jubilee, California, USA (1979)

Sacramento Jazz Festival, California, USA (1980, 1981, 1982)
Sacramento Jazz Festival, California, USA (1985, 1986, 1987, 1988)
Chilliwack Jazz Festival, Canada (1989)

Sacramento Jubilee, California, USA (1991)
Sacramento Jubilee, California, USA (1993)
Moodus Jazz Festival, Connecticut, USA (1995)
Sacramento Jubilee, California, USA (1996)
Sacramento Jubilee, California, USA (1999)
Golden Jubilee Party, Crowne Plaza Hotel, Liverpool (1999)

APPENDIX 3

THE MERSEYSIPPI JAZZ BAND - DISCOGRAPHY

Singles (10)

Unlike pop records, there were no nominated A or B sides on these singles. The record companies chose tracks which sounded compatible together.
Friendless Blues / Moose March (Decibel SJ 101) (1952) (Only 99 copies pressed)
Big Bear Stomp / Daddy Do (Esquire 10-418) (1954)
Aunt Hagar's Blues / Jersey Lightning (Esquire 10-428) (1955)
Swipesy Cake Walk / Whitewash Man (Esquire 10-438) (1955)
Creole Love Call / Hiawatha (Esquire 10-448) (1955)
Blues Doctor / Chicago Buzz (Esquire 10-478) (1956)
Ostrich Walk / Saturday Night Function (Esquire 10-486) (1956)
Très Moutarde / Weather Bird Rag (Esquire 10-492) (1956)
Funky Butt / New Rag (Oriole 45CB 1593) (1961)
Oh By Jingo / Get Out And Get Under (Both with Clinton Ford) (Oriole 45CB 1612) (1961)

Extended Plays (7)

JAZZ PLAYED BY JAZZ BANDS, VOLUME 3 (Esquire EP 30) (1955)
The Mooche
Sage Hen Strut

THE MERSEYSIPPI JAZZ BAND AT THE ROYAL FESTIVAL HALL (Decca DFE 6251) (1955)
Creole Belles
Creole Love Call
Whitewash Man
Snake Rag

JAZZ PLAYED BY JAZZ BANDS, VOLUME 7 (Esquire EP 60) (1955)
Black And Tan Fantasy
Emperor Norton's Hunch

JAZZ PLAYED BY JAZZ BANDS, VOLUME 13 (Esquire EP 90)
(1955)
That's A Plenty
Memphis Blues

JAZZ PLAYED BY JAZZ BANDS, VOLUME 16 (Esquire EP 118)
(1955)
Hiawatha
Creole Love Call
Swipesy Cake Walk
Whitewash Man

JAZZ PLAYED BY JAZZ BANDS, VOLUME 23 (Esquire EP 130)
(1955)
Chicago Buzz
Blues Doctor
Grandpa's Spells
Working Man Blues

CLINTON FORD GOES TRADITIONAL (Oriole EP 7027) (1960)
I Wish I Was In Peoria
Get Out And Get Under
Oh, By Jingo!
Wana

Albums (21)

TRADITIONAL JAZZ SCENE, 1955 (12 inch LP, Decca LK 4100)
(1955)
Recorded at Royal Festival Hall, London under the auspices of the
National Jazz Federation
Featuring Merseysippi Jazz Band, Chris Barber's Jazz Band with
Ottilie Patterson, Zenith Six, Alex Welsh Dixielanders with George
Melly and Roy Crimmins
Creole Belles (Correct title is 'Creole Belle')
Young Woman's Blues (with Beryl Bryden)

THE MERSEYSIPPI JAZZ BAND (10 inch LP, Deroy ADM 118)
(1955)
That's A Plenty
Copenhagen

166

Get Out Of Here And Go On Home
Basin Street Blues
St Louis Blues
Royal Garden Blues
Fidgety Feet
1919 March

WEST COAST SHOUT (10 inch LP, Esquire 20 -063) (1956)
West Coast Shout
Weather Bird Rag
Ostrich Walk
Saturday Night Function
Très Moutarde
Sidewalk Blues

ALL THE GIRLS (10 inch LP, Esquire 20-083) (1957)
All The Girls
Mabel's Dream
When You And I Were Young, Maggie
Sweet Lorraine
Annie Street Rock
Mandy Lee Blues
Sweet Georgia Brown
Dinah Lou
All The Girls

MERSEY TUNNEL JAZZ (10 inch LP, Esquire 20-088) (1957)
Kansas City Stomps
Bienville Blues
Duff Campbell's Revenge
My Journey To The Sky
Hop Frog
If I Had You
Cataract Rag
I'm Gonna Sit Right Down And Write Myself A Letter

ANY OLD RAGS (10 inch LP, Esquire 20-093) (1958)
Original Rag
Trombone Rag
Hysterics Rag
Ragtime Goblin Man

Eccentric Rag
Panama Rag
Alexander's Ragtime Band
Bees Knees

VOLUME 1: THE DUCK IN FLIGHT (LP, Ribbet KM 4904) (1979)
The sub-titles of Volumes 1 and 2 relate to what you can do with your private parts - or so I'm told.
King Porter Stomp
Someday You'll Be Sorry
Jelly Bean Blues
Working Man Blues
Gimme A Pigfoot (And A Bottle Of Beer)
My Journey To The Sky
Swing That Music
Careless Love Blues
The Right Key But The Wrong Keyhole
Chimes Blues
Potato Head Blues
Goodbye Dolly Gray

VOLUME 2: MAN, WOMAN AND BULLDOG (LP, Ribbet KM 6433) (1981)
Hop Frog
Do Your Duty
Creole Belles
Million Dollar Secret
Original Rags
Henry Hudson
Oriental Strut
I've Got What It Takes
Smoky Mokes
Ory's Creole Trombone
Cakewalkin' Babies From Home

THE MERSEYSIPPI JAZZ BAND WITH JAN SUTHERLAND LIVE AT HOLLY LODGE (LP, Swallow SWS 203) (1982)
"This was meant to be Volume 3" says John Lawrence, "but we were very casual about these things."
Yellow Dog Blues
South

A Hundred Years From Today
The Tattooed Lady
Wolverine Blues
You've Been A Good Old Wagon
Sailing Down The Chesapeake Bay
Trombone Cholly
Chastity Belt
Sage Hen Strut

OH, YOU CALIFORNIA (12 inch LP, Ribbet / Sun Coast SCR 104) (1985)
Oh, You California (with Clinton Ford)
Whitewash Man
Get Out And Get Under (with Clinton Ford)
Funky Butt
Muddy Water (with Clinton Ford)
Emperor Norton's Hunch
My Cutey's Due At 2.22 (with Clinton Ford)
Chicago Buzz
Mandy, Make Up Your Mind (with Clinton Ford)
Cornet Chop Suey
Bedelia (with Clinton Ford)
Once In A While

OH YOU CALIFORNIA (Cassette, Ribbet / Sun Coast RTS 822) (1985)
As above plus
Doodle-doo-doo (with Clinton Ford)
Singin' The Blues

BACK TO SQUARE ONE (Cassette, no number shown) (1987)
I'm Gonna Meet My Sweetie Now
Clementine (From New Orleans)
Beale Street Mama
Chattanooga Stomp
I'm A Little Blackbird
Cataract Rag
Don't Monkey With It
Jersey Lightning
Grandpa's Spells
Annie Street Rock

All Night Blues
Dapper Dan
Friendless Blues
Hindustan

UP THE AMAZON (Cassette, MJB 3) (1988)
Panama Rag
Since My Best Girl Turned Me Down
East St Louis Toodle-oo
Swipesy Cake Walk
Minstrels Of Annie Street
Do You Know What It Means To Miss New Orleans
Hysterics Rag
The Song Of Leningrad
Clarinet Marmalade
Snag It
Sidewalk Blues
Corn Silk
Sweet Georgia Brown
Some Day Sweetheart
Big Bear Stomp

SWEEPING THE BLUES AWAY (Cassette, MJB4) (1990)
I've Found A New Baby
I'm Coming Virginia
Dill Pickles
Sweeping The Blues Away
Oh Marie
Trombone Rag
Sweet Mama
Kansas City Stomps
Weary Blues
Lonesome
New Rags
Black And Tan Fantasy
The Lonesomest Gal In Town
Tin Roof Blues
Flat Foot
Wolverine Blues

A DIP IN THE MERSEY (CD & Cassette, MJB CD/P5 & C/P5)

(1993)
Sunset Café Stomp
Chimes Blues
If Someone Would Only Love Me
I'm Going Away To Wear You Off My Mind
Sweet Like This
Mandy Lee Blues
Sister Salvation
Oh, But On The Third Day
The Chant
Cleopatra's Blues
Huggin' And Chalkin'
Duff Campbell's Revenge
Of All The Wrongs You've Done To Me
Shake It And Break It
Misty Morning
You're Driving Me Crazy
Saloon

HAPPY HOUR (Cassette, MJB C/P6) (1996)
Sailing Down The Chesapeake Bay
On The Sunny Side Of The Street
Down Among The Sheltering Palms
My Little Bimbo
Lazy River
The Lion And Albert
The Return Of Albert
Never Swat A Fly
My Grandad's Flannelette Night Shirt
I Wish I Could Shimmy Like My Sister Kate
Coney Island Washboard
Waiting For The Robert E. Lee
I'm Getting Sentimental Over You
Gunner Joe
The Battle Of Hastings
Rose Of Washington Square
My Little Stick Of Blackpool Rock
Oh By Jingo
Ugly Child
All By Myself
Ev'rything Is Peaches Down In Georgia

Doin' The New Lowdown
Sweethearts On Parade

THE QUALITY OF MERSEY (CD & Cassette, MJB CD/P7 & C/P7)
(1996)
West Coast Shout
Henry Hudson
Creole Love Call
I Wish I Was In Peoria
Working Man Blues
Smoky Mokes
Original Rags
Hop Frog
Savoy Blues
How Can You Face Me
Bad Penny Blues
I'm Going Back To Bottomland
The Thin Red Line
Memphis Blues
Original Dixieland One Step

**THE BEST OF BRITISH JAZZ FROM THE BBC JAZZ CLUB,
VOLUME 6** (CD, Upbeat URCD 127) (1997)
Two performances from 1959
I'm Coming Virginia
Creole Belles

**MERSEY TUNNEL JAZZ - MERSEYSIPPI JAZZ BAND 1954-
1957** (CD, Lake LACD 85) (1997)
CD combines the whole of 'West Coast Shout' and 'Mersey Tunnel
Jazz' plus
Jersey Lightning
Aunt Hagar's Blues
Black And Tan Fantasy
Emperor Norton's Hunch
Chicago Buzz
Blues Doctor

SENIOR MOMENTS (CD, Lake LACD 113) (1999)
Moose March
Bees Knees

I Can't Believe That You're In Love With Me
Melancholy Blues
Alexander's Ragtime Band (with Clinton Ford)
Gimme A Pigfoot (And A Bottle Of Beer)
Copenhagen
Big Fat Ham
Where Did You Stay Last Night
Sailing On The Robert E. Lee
There'll Come A Time
Ory's Creole Trombone
Hesitating Blues
Sorry
Aunt Hagar's Blues
My Baby's Wild About My Old Trombone
My Heart

THE GREAT REVIVAL, VOLUME 4 (Lake LACD 137) (2001)
Compilation with three titles from Esquire catalogue:
Big Bear Stomp
Daddy Do
Sage Hen Strut

TICKETS PRICE 12/6 FOR THE......

ALL NIGHT HAPPENING
12 Hour Rave Starting 7 p.m. on

SATURDAY, 10th. JUNE 1967

At Liverpool's World-Famous

CAVERN CLUB

Appearing on Stage will be
BONZO ˙DOG DOO DAH BAND ● ESCORTS
SCAFFOLD ● KLUBS ● BRIAN PATTERN
MERSEYSIPPI JAZZ BAND

"THROUGH THE LOOKING GLASS" FASHION PARADE
Compers: BOB WOOLER - BILLY BUTLER - RON PIMLETT
BIG TAMLA DISC SHOW - SNACKS ETC.

— LATE LICENSED BARS —

091   Proceeds in aid of North East Liverpool Technical
      College, July Sahara Expedition.

I COULD WRITE A BOOK

The following publications were consulted in researching 'Sweeping The Blues Away':

Bielderman, Gerard	Eurojazz Discos No.60 - Merseysippi Jazz Band	(Gerard Bielderman, 1997)
Carr, Ian & Others	Jazz: The Essential Companion	(Paladin, 1988)
Chilton, John	Jazz	(Teach Yourself Books, 1979)
Chilton, John	Who's Who Of British Jazz	(Cassell, 1997)
Davies, Hunter	The Quarrymen	(Omnibus, 2001)
Erlewine, Michael & Others	All Music Guide To Jazz	(Miller Freeman, 1998)
Fordham, John	Let's Join Hands And Contact The Living - Ronnie Scott And His Club	(Elm Tree, 1986)
Fox, Charles & Others	Jazz On Record - A Critical Guide	(Arrow, 1960)
Godbolt, Jim	A History Of Jazz In Britain, 1919-50	(Quartet, 1984)
Melly, George	Mellymobile	(Robson, 1982)
Melly, George	Owning-Up	(Weidenfeld & Nicolson, 1965)
Merseysippi Jazz Band	Eight To The Bar For Fifty Years	(Commemorative booklet, 1999)

Spencer Leigh was born in Liverpool in 1945. His "On The Beat" programme has been broadcast on BBC Radio Merseyside for over 15 years and he has written for several magazines including "Country Music People", "Now Dig This", "Record Buyer", "Record Collector" and "Radio Times". He also writes obituaries for "The Independent" so he is often tempted to offer musicians a complete package of radio interview, magazine article and forthcoming obituary.

Spencer Leigh's books are "Paul Simon - Now And Then" (1973), "Presley Nation" (1976), "Stars In My Eyes" (1980), "Let's Go Down The Cavern" (with Pete Frame) (1984), "Speaking Words Of Wisdom: Reflections On The Beatles" (1991), "Aspects Of Elvis" (edited with Alan Clayson) (1994), "Memories Of Buddy Holly" (with Jim Dawson) (US only, 1996), "Halfway To Paradise, Britpop 1955 - 1962" (with John Firminger) (1996), "Behind The Song" (with Michael Heatley) (1998), "Drummed Out - The Sacking Of Pete Best" (1998), "Brother, Can You Spare A Rhyme? - 100 Years Of Hit Songwriting" (2000) and "Baby, That Is Rock And Roll, American Pop 1954 - 1963" (2001). He comments, "This is my thirteenth book so it's lucky I'm not the slightest bit superstitious."